THE MYSTERY OF CHRIST

Life in Death

The Mystery of Christ

LIFE IN DEATH

John Behr

ST VLADIMIR'S SEMINARY PRESS
CRESTWOOD, NEW YORK

Library of Congress Cataloging-in-Publication Data

Behr, John.
The mystery of Christ : life in death / John Behr
p. cm.
Includes index.
ISBN-13: 978–0–88141–306–9 (alk. paper)
ISBN-10: 0–88141–306–2 (alk. paper)
1. Theology, Doctrinal—History—Early church, ca. 30–600. 2. Jesus Christ—History of doctrines—Early church, ca. 30–600. I. Title.
BT23.B46 2006
230—dc22

2005032932

Permission for use of the following images has been granted by:

Plate 1: Illustration of the Crucifixion of the Living Christ, Scala/Art Resource.

Plate 2: The Creation, Scala/Art Resource.

Plate 3: The Anastasis (Resurrection) of Christ, St Vladimir's Seminary Press.

Plate 4: The Virgin Orans and Christ Child, Scala/Art Resource.

Plate 5: Icon with the Crucifixion and Nativity, The Holy Monastery of Saint Catherine, Sinai, Egypt. Photograph by Bruce White. Photograph © 2003 The Metropolitan Museum of Art.

ST VLADIMIR'S SEMINARY PRESS
575 Scarsdale Rd, Crestwood, NY 10707
1-800-204-2665
www.svspress.com

ISBN 978–0–88141–306–9

PRINTED IN CANADA

Through him you sought us when we were not seeking you,
but you sought us that we might begin to seek you.

St Augustine

We only understand life backwards, but we must live forwards.

Søren Kierkegaard

For Claudia

Table of Contents

List of Plates

Abbreviations

ACW	Ancient Christian Writers
ANF	The Ante-Nicene Fathers (Edinburgh, 1885ff; frequently reprinted and now available at many sites on the World Wide Web)
CCSG	Corpus Christianorum, Series Graeca
CS	Cistercian Studies
CSCO	Corpus Scriptorum Christianorum Orientalium
CWS	Classics of Western Spirituality
FC	The Fathers of the Church
GCS	Die griechischen christlichen Schriftsteller der ersten drei Jahrhunderte
GNO	Gregorii Nysseni Opera
LCL	Loeb Classical Library
NPNF	The Nicene and Post-Nicene Fathers, two series (New York, 1887–92; Oxford 1890–1900; frequently reprinted and now available at many sites on the World Wide Web)
OECT	Oxford Early Christian Texts
PG	Patrologia Graeca (Paris, 1857–66)
PTS	Patristische Texte und Studien
SC	Sources Chrétiennes

We only understand life backwards, but we must live forwards.

Søren Kierkegaard

Preface

This book provides an account of Christian theology that is systematic yet remains true to the way in which theology was first learned. This is not as simple as it might seem, but it is a task worth undertaking. As we turn again to the early witnesses, we will be challenged to rethink our approach to theology, its vocabulary, and the manner in which we read scripture. Yet we will also find a vision that might seem radical, even extraordinarily daring, but which far surpasses our limited modern scope in both breadth and vitality.

Most modern expositions of theology exemplify Kierkegaard's observation, that we understand backwards, yet fail to take adequate account of this fact. That is, they begin with the results of the theological debates of the early centuries—especially Trinitarian theology and Christology—but separate these theological formulas from the way in which they were in fact learned and from the exegetical practice, the manner of using scripture, in and through which they were articulated. Starting with detached theological formulas, a doctrine of the being of God, as Trinity, is posited, and then scripture is read in a distinctively modern manner, as a history of the interaction between God and the world: the Creation, the life of Adam and Eve in Paradise, the Fall, the long history of salvation, in which God (usually in the person of the "preincarnate Logos") appeared to Abraham and spoke with Moses and through the Prophets, culminating in the work of salvation when the Son became incarnate and, after the Passion, returned to the Father, sending the Spirit to guide the Church through the remaining time of human history until the Second Coming.

Such an approach to theology has become, in modern times, all but ubiquitous. But the fact that we only understand retrospectively should caution us to consider more carefully how such theological statements are made and what kind of assertions they are. For example, in the above approach, the term "Incarnation" is used to refer to the becoming human of the second person of the Trinity by being born from the Virgin Mary. But it is a stubborn fact, or at least is presented this way in the Gospels of Matthew, Mark, and Luke, that the one born of Mary was not known by the disciples to be the Son of God until after the Passion, his crucifixion and resurrection (the apparent exception, Peter's confession in Mt 16, in fact proves the point, and the Gospel of John takes this reflection further, as we will see). Thus, to speak of the "Incarnation," to say that the one born of the Virgin is the Son of God, is an *interpretation* made only in the light of the Passion. It is a *confession* about the crucified and exalted Lord, whose birth is then described in terms drawn from the account of his death (the correspondence between the tomb and the womb that delighted early Christians and is celebrated in liturgical texts and iconography); it is not a neutral statement that could be verified by an uninvolved bystander as part of an objective history, an account of things "as they actually happened," in the manner of nineteenth-century historiography. Although popular imagination is still enthralled by the idea of "what really happened," it is generally recognized today that there is no such thing as uninterpreted history. Failing to appreciate the confessional nature of theological assertions gives much modern theology a character that can only be described as an odd mixture of metaphysics and mythology.

The interpretative character of theological statements forces us to take seriously the exegetical practices of the apostles and the early Christians following in their footsteps, in and through which doctrinal formulas were articulated. The disciples did not simply come to understand Christ in the light of the Passion. Rather, only when turned again (or were turned by the risen Christ) to the scriptures (meaning what we now call the "Old Testament") did they began to see there all sorts of references to Christ, and specifically to the necessity that he should suffer before entering his glory (cf. Lk 24.27), which they then used in their proclamation of Christ. In other words, the scriptures were not used merely as a narrative of the past, but rather as a thesaurus, a treasury of imagery, for entering into the mystery of Christ, the starting point for which is the historical event of the Passion. In this it is not so much scripture that is being exegeted, but rather Christ who is being interpreted by recourse to the scriptures. Not that they denied that God had been at work in the past, but their account of this "salvation history" is one which is told from the perspective of their encounter with the risen Lord, seeing him as providentially arranging the whole economy, the "plan of salvation," such that it culminates in him.

It is sometimes said that for antiquity truth is what *is*, for enlightened modernity it is what *was*, and for postmodernity it is *that which will have been*. The historicizing approach of modernity places the truth of Jesus Christ firmly in the past—how he was born and what he did and said—and subjects his truth to our criteria of historicity, which are ultimately no more than a matter of what we find plausible (as is evidenced by the "Jesus Seminar"). For antiquity, on the other hand, the truth of Christ is eternal, or better, timeless: the crucified and risen Lord is the one of whom scripture has always spoken. Yet, as the disciples come to recognize him, as the subject of scripture and in the breaking of bread, he disappears from their sight (Lk 24.31). The Christ of Christian faith, revealed concretely in and through the apostolic proclamation of the crucified and risen Lord in accordance with scripture, is an eschatological figure, the Coming One. Hence the importance of the other half of Kierkegaard's observation, that while we understand retrospectively, we nevertheless live into the future. As we leave behind modernity's fascination with the past, it is possible that we are once again in a position to recognize the eschatological Lord.

This, moreover, allows us to see a greater depth of meaning in the term "Incarnation." As it is only in the light of the Passion that we can even speak of "Incarnation," the sense of this term is pregnant with a greater fertility: by the proclamation of his gospel, the apostle Paul is in travail giving birth to Christ in those who receive his gospel (cf. Gal 4.19), that is, who accept the interpretation he offers in accordance with scripture, and are thereby born again to be the body of Christ. This is still in process, as our life is "hidden with Christ in God" (Col 3.3). Yet the indeterminacy celebrated by post-modernism, locating the "event" always in the future, is given concrete content in Christian theology, by anchoring its account in the crucial moment of the Passion. The timeless subject of Christian theology is the crucified and risen Lord, the one who "was from the beginning, [who] appeared new yet is found to be old, and is ever young, being born in the hearts of the saints."[1]

The historical approach of modernity has resulted in the discipline of theology becoming increasingly fragmented. Students of scripture, historical theology, and systematic theology have each pursued their own disciplines, in ways that make them increasingly unable to dialogue with each other, so that it is difficult to see them as belonging to the same pursuit: the study of scripture has, until recently, been dominated by the presuppositions of a historical-critical method—looking for the original text, its context and redaction, and its interpretation (in terms of what it *meant* rather than *means*); the study of the Fathers has focused on the development of doctrine that is already supposedly known, treating patristic exegesis as if it were a distinct subject, and is increasingly turning to any subject other than theology, becoming the study of Late Antiquity rather than Patristics; and systematic theology—working with the results of earlier studies in historical theology, overlooking the exegetical dimension of patristic theology, and looking askance at modern scriptural scholarship—has become burdened by the momentum of its own discourse to become increasingly self-reflexive, concerned with its own methodology. The reappropriation of a premodern perspective in a cautious postmodern fashion, such as that offered in this book, might point a way out of the quandary in which theology has found itself in recent centuries, and forward to a space in which we can appreciate again the integrity and unity of the discipline of theology, and see anew its vision.

Given these considerations, it will come as no surprise that the account of Christian theology given here does not proceed in the customary manner as sketched above. Rather, the book begins with the way in which the disciples of Christ came to know him as the Son of God, that is, through the Cross and the manner in which the Passion is interpreted and Christ proclaimed. Chapter Two examines further this exegetical approach and framework, considering questions such as canon and tradition. Chapter Three then looks at how, in this perspective, we speak of creation and salvation, what is meant (and not meant) by the "Fall," and at how salvation history is narrated, not only that presented by scripture, but also more globally in world history, and more particularly in our own lives. Chapter Four turns to the subject of the birth of Christ, and the Church as the Virgin Mother, the one in whom Christians are born again and Christ born in them, and how the Virgin Mary is spoken of in the Gospels and liturgical texts. Chapter Five continues this theme of "Incarnation" by focusing on the body, and its ambiguity (again the need for interpretation), as that in which Christians are to glorify God. Finally, the Postscript offers a sketch of the paradigm shift implied by a postmodern reappropriation of a premodern perspective and some further considerations.

The vision of theology offered in this book is based on my earlier works, *The Way to Nicaea* and *The Nicene Faith*, which examine in detail the key figures of the first four centuries.[2] These two books are the first volumes of a series, The Formation of Christian Theology, which will continue to the Seventh Ecumenical Council—an arbitrary terminus, but one has to stop somewhere, and this period covers a history common to East and West. The series is not yet complete, but it seemed desirable even at this stage to offer a systematic presentation of the theology that has emerged from this work. For further details, and more concrete sketches of the particular theological vision of each figure treated, recourse to these books (if not to the primary texts themselves) may be made. It remains for me to thank all those who have commented on the earlier works and all those who have read through this present volume and offered valuable suggestions.

NOTES

[1] *The Epistle to Diognetus* 11. Ed. and trans. K. Lake, LCL The Apostolic Fathers 2 (Cambridge, MA: Harvard University Press, 1976 [1913]).

[2] J. Behr, *The Way to Nicaea* (Crestwood, NY: St Vladimir's Seminary Press, 2001); *The Nicene Faith* (Crestwood, NY: St Vladimir's Seminary Press, 2004).

CHAPTER ONE

Through the Cross

ENCOUNTERING CHRIST

Probably the most striking aspect about the first three Gospels, their description of the life of Christ and his dealings with his disciples, is that although the disciples accompanied Christ for a period of time, although they saw him working miracles and transfigured on the mountain of Tabor, and although they heard all sorts of divine teachings from him, they all abandoned him at the time of his crucifixion. In the Gospel of John it is otherwise, and this is a difference to which we will return at the end of this chapter. But in the Synoptic Gospels, those of Matthew, Mark, and Luke, the disciples abandon Christ—Peter even denies ever having known him! How can this be? How is it that they did not understand who he is?

As they continued to meet, fearfully and secretly, others began to persecute them, just as Christ had been persecuted. Most notable among the persecutors, of course, was Saul, later to become the apostle Paul. The book of Acts describes how while Saul was journeying to Damascus, he was struck down by a flash of light and heard the words: "Saul, Saul, why are you persecuting me?" (Acts 9.4). When Saul asked who it was who said this, he heard: "I am Jesus, whom you are persecuting." Jesus identifies himself with the persecuted Church, his body, and just as it is the victim Jesus who returns to his judges as their Savior, so it is through one of the members of the persecuted body of Christ, Ananias, that Saul is baptized, receiving back his sight, and then, as the apostle Paul, proclaiming Christ on his missionary journeys.

In the apostle Paul's letters, which were written before any of the evangelists composed their Gospels, we have the earliest statements of the Christian faith. Perhaps the most important such statement comes in the First Letter to the Corinthians:

> I delivered to you as of first importance what I also received, that Christ died for our sins in accordance with the scriptures, and that he was buried and that he was raised on the third day in accordance with the scriptures, and that he appeared to Cephas, then to the twelve. (1 Cor 15.3–5)

What is most important here is the phrase that the apostle Paul repeats twice: Christ died and rose "in accordance with the scriptures." This phrase is so important that it is preserved in the Nicene-Constantinopolitan Creed which is still said at every Orthodox Christian baptism and celebration of the Divine Liturgy: Christ died and rose in accordance with the (same) scriptures. It is important to recognize that the scriptures in question are not the Gospels—Matthew, Mark, Luke, and John—they had not even been written when Paul made this statement, but rather what we now call the Old Testament—the Law, the Psalms, and the Prophets.

So, despite having been with Christ for a number of years, having heard his words and seen his marvelous actions, the disciples did not yet really understand him. Only after his Passion, his crucifixion and exaltation, do they begin to understand who Christ is and what he has done, and they did this by turning back to the scriptures. Speaking of Christ's entry into Jerusalem, John comments that "his disciples did not understand this at first; but when Jesus was glorified, then they remembered that this had been written of him and had been done to him" (Jn 12.16). In their subsequent proclamation of the mystery of Christ, the apostles and evangelists continued to use the terms and images provided by these scriptures to describe the work of God in Christ. Sometimes this is made explicit, and occasionally Christ himself is presented as using the words of scripture to explain who he is and what work he has come to fulfill, as, for instance, when, in the Gospel of John, he says:

> "As Moses lifted up the serpent in the wilderness, so must the Son of man be lifted up, that whoever believes in him may have eternal life." (Jn 3.14–15)

Christ is referring back to the book of Numbers. There, when the Israelites complained to Moses that it was folly to remain in the desert—the wisdom of the world arguing that it is preferable to go back to Egypt—God struck the people with the deadly bites of serpents and, at the same time, provided a remedy: the bronze serpent was lifted up on a pole. By looking upon the serpent, the people regained life (Num 21.4–9). Paul also appeals to this imagery, when he points out to those in his Corinthian community who were seduced by worldly wisdom, that the folly of God (Christ lifted on the cross, as the bronze snake lifted on the pole) overcomes the wisdom of the world, and, as such, Christ is the true power and wisdom of God (1 Cor 1.22–5). And, as this is his message, the apostle emphasizes that he does not preach in words that might appear powerful in worldly terms, but in a manner that seems foolish by worldly standards—for it is in such foolishness that the strength of God is manifest:

> When I came to you, brethren, I did not come proclaiming to you the testimony of God in lofty words or wisdom. For I decided to know nothing among you except Jesus Christ and him crucified. And I was with you in weakness and in much fear and trembling; and my speech and my message were not in plausible words of wisdom, but in demonstration of the Spirit and of power, that your faith might not rest in the wisdom of men but in the power of God. (1 Cor 2.1–6)

There are many images in the Old Testament, besides the bronze serpent, which the apostles used to understand the Passion of Christ. For instance, Abraham offered his beloved son Isaac in obedience to God (Gen 22), an offering which God did not ultimately allow to be given, but in turn offers his only-begotten Son for us. Another important image is the lamb slain at the time of the exodus from Egypt, the blood of which the Israelites smeared over the doors of their dwellings so that the angel of death would pass over their houses and not take their first-born sons (Ex 12).

These same passages and others like them are used even now during the Holy Week services of the Orthodox Church, especially on Holy Friday and at the vesperal Divine Liturgy of Holy Saturday (often celebrated in the morning), during which fifteen Old Testament passages are read. These readings are not read simply as reports about things that happened a long time ago and that in some way anticipate the Passion of Christ. Rather, these key testimonies of scripture were considered by the apostles and the early Christians, and still are by those who celebrate these services now, as speaking directly about Christ, offering us insights into the mystery of the Lord's Passion.

That these passages are taken as referring directly to the Passion is made clear by Melito of Sardis, in his work *On Pascha*, written sometime in the late second century. This is a liturgical homily, delivered on the night of the celebration of Pascha. It begins just after the passage from Exodus about the slain lambs and the flight from Egypt has been read out, and continues by expounding the scriptures, culminating in an early form of the Eucharist and with Melito speaking in the person of the Risen Christ. After speaking at length about how the angel of death killed all the first born sons of the Egyptians, but left the Israelites alone, Melito asks the angel:

32) Tell me angel, what turned you away?
The slaughter of the sheep or the life of the Lord?
The death of the sheep or the type of the Lord?
The blood of the sheep or the spirit of the Lord?

33) It is clear that you turned away
seeing the mystery of the Lord in the sheep
and the life of the Lord in the slaughter of the sheep
and the type of the Lord in the death of the sheep.
Therefore you struck not Israel down,
but made Egypt alone childless.[1]

The angel of death turned away from the Israelites, according to Melito, not because of the sheep's blood itself, but because he already saw in the blood a sign of "the mystery of the Lord." Melito then continues by speaking of other images by which scripture speaks of Christ, and exhorts us:

59) Thus if you wish to see the mystery of the Lord
look at Abel who is likewise slain,
at Isaac who is likewise tied up,
at Joseph who is likewise traded,
at Moses who is likewise exposed,
at David who is likewise hunted down,
at the prophets who likewise suffer for the sake of Christ.

In many ways, then, scripture, the Old Testament, provided the means by which the disciples began to understand how God was at work in the Passion of Christ.

In their Gospels, the evangelists used these images to describe not only the death of Christ but going further back, his birth and life, and also their encounter with the risen Lord. When the risen Jesus accompanied the two disciples on the road to Emmaus, they did not immediately recognize him. The two disciples mention that they had hoped that Jesus was the one who was going to redeem Israel, but that he had instead been put to death. They also relate that when some women of their company went to the tomb, they found it empty. Even at this point they still don't get it! And so Christ reproves them:

> "O foolish men, and slow of heart to believe all that the prophets have spoken! Was it not necessary that the Christ should suffer these things and enter into his glory?" And beginning with Moses and all the prophets, he interpreted to them in all the scriptures the things concerning himself. (Lk 24.25–27, see also 44–47)

Without any other comment, Luke continues by describing how these two disciples persuaded Christ to stay the evening with them and how their eyes were opened in the breaking of the bread. But as soon as they recognized him, he disappeared from their sight, so that they were left reflecting on what had happened, saying to each other "did not our hearts burn within us, while he talked to us on the road, while he opened to us the scriptures?" (Lk 24.32). That the risen Christ disappeared from their sight, coming and going as he pleases, demonstrates how he is no longer subject to the temporal, spatial, and material constrictions of this world, reminding us, as the apostle Paul put it, that we no longer know Christ after the flesh, but according to the Spirit (2 Cor 5.16), a point to which we will return.

In Christ's own words, then, it was necessary that he should suffer these things. This point is made even on the sole occasion before the Passion when one of the disciples recognizes who Jesus truly is. When Peter confesses that he is "the Christ, the Son of the living God" (Mt 16.16), Jesus replies by pointing out that Peter did not know this "by flesh and blood"—by Peter's human contact with Jesus—but by a revelation granted by the heavenly Father. Then, on the basis of this confession,

Christ establishes the apostle Peter, the rock, as the foundation of the Church. However, when Christ then reveals to his disciples that he must go to Jerusalem to suffer and be put to death, Peter begins to protest: "This shall never happen to you!" and receives the most damning words from the lips of Jesus: "Get behind me Satan! You are a hindrance to me; for you are not on the side of God, but of men!" (Mt 16.23). The apostle who has just been recognized as the foundation of the Church is now called Satan by Christ, for trying to prevent him from going to his Passion. Following the words of Christ here, one might say that Satan is the one who gets between Christ and his Cross.

Most important in what we have seen so far is *how* it was that the disciples came to know that Jesus is the Lord, the Son of God. They did not come to this knowledge through hearing reports about his birth nor by accompanying him for a period of time. This simply reflects the fact that the usual methods of human knowledge—scientific analysis, historical inquiry, or philosophical reflection—are inadequate when the desired object of knowledge is God, for God is not subject to human perception, whether physical or mental, but shows himself as and when he wills, just as the risen Christ comes and goes at his own pleasure and, as we have seen, disappears from sight once he is recognized. Yet neither was it merely seeing Christ on the cross that prompted the disciples, finally, to know the Lord, nor even was the report about the empty tomb or the encounter with the risen Christ enough to persuade the disciples: the tomb is empty, but this in itself is ambiguous, and when he appears, he is not immediately recognized.

Rather, the disciples came to recognize the Lord as the one whose Passion is spoken of by the scriptures and encountered him in the breaking of bread. It is these two complementary ways, the engagement with the scriptures and sharing in the Lord's meal, "proclaiming his death until he comes" (1 Cor 11.26), that Paul specifies he had received (from the Lord himself in the case of the eucharistic meal) and then handed down, or "traditioned," to later generations (cf. 1 Cor 11.23, 15.3). These constitute, as it were, the matrix and the sustenance of the Christian tradition. From this vantage point, we can now look back to the Cross, the last publicly visible image (the tomb, after all, was empty and seen only by a few, and the risen Christ disappears from our sight when he is recognized), as the sign of victory, as we await the return of the Lord; as the apostle Paul said, he would preach nothing else but Christ and him crucified. The images throughout the early Christian period depicting the Crucifixion, such as that in the Rabbula Gospels (Plate 1), consistently depict the crucified Christ with an upright body and eyes wide open, not because of an inability to depict a dead corpse, but precisely because the crucified one is the triumphant Lord: the Cross itself is taken simultaneously as a reference to the Crucifixion and to the risen Christ.[2] The Christ that Christians are concerned with is always the crucified and exalted one, the one who has now entered into his glory.

THE VOLUNTARY SUFFERING OF THE INNOCENT VICTIM

We have seen a number of passages from the Old Testament which were used by the apostles in their attempt to understand and proclaim Christ, but not the one which is probably the most important and certainly the most moving. This is what is sometimes called the fourth song of the Suffering Servant:

> Behold, my servant shall prosper, he shall be exalted and lifted up, and shall be very high.
>
> As many were astonished at him—his appearance was so marred, beyond human semblance, and his form beyond that of the sons of men—
>
> so shall he startle many nations; kings shall shut their mouths because of him; for that which has not been told them they shall see, and that which they have not heard they shall understand.

Who has believed what we have heard? And to whom has the arm of the LORD been revealed?

For he grew up before him like a young plant, and like a root out of dry ground; he had no form or comeliness that we should look at him, and no beauty that we should desire him.

He was despised and rejected by men; a man of sorrows, and acquainted with grief; and as one from whom men hide their faces he was despised, and we esteemed him not.

Surely he has borne our griefs and carried our sorrows; yet we esteemed him stricken, smitten by God, and afflicted.

But he was wounded for our transgressions, he was bruised for our iniquities; upon him was the chastisement that made us whole, and with his stripes we are healed.

All we like sheep have gone astray; we have turned every one to his own way; and the LORD has laid on him the iniquity of us all.

He was oppressed, and he was afflicted, yet he opened not his mouth; like a lamb that is led to the slaughter, and like a sheep that before its shearers is dumb, so he opened not his mouth.

By oppression and judgment he was taken away; and as for his generation, who considered that he was cut off out of the land of the living, stricken for the transgression of my people?

And they made his grave with the wicked and with a rich man in his death, although he had done no violence, and there was no deceit in his mouth.

Yet it was the will of the LORD to bruise him; he has put him to grief; when he makes himself an offering for sin, he shall see his offspring, he shall prolong his days; the will of the LORD shall prosper in his hand; he shall see the fruit of the travail of his soul and be satisfied; by his knowledge shall the righteous one, my servant, make many to be accounted righteous; and he shall bear their iniquities.

Therefore I will divide him a portion with the great, and he shall divide the spoil with the strong; because he poured out his soul to

> death, and was numbered with the transgressors; yet he bore the sin of many, and made intercession for the transgressors. (Is 52.13–53.12)

Not surprisingly, this passage nourished reflection on the person and work of Jesus Christ from the beginning. The images it uses are already present in the Gospel accounts of the Passion. The manner in which the apostle Peter paraphrased the passage indicates clearly what was understood to be its central affirmation:

> He committed no sin; no guile was found on his lips. When he was reviled, he did not revile in return; when he suffered, he did not threaten; but trusted to him who judges justly. He bore our sins in his body on the tree, that we might die to sin and live to righteousness. (1 Pet 2.22–24)

In and through the sufferings we inflict, Christ does not condemn, resist, or exclude; he suffers violence, but never inflicts it: he is the lamb who takes upon himself the sin of the world. What is most moving and poignant about the passage from Isaiah, the insight taken up by the apostles, is that Christ went voluntarily to the cross, as innocent as a lamb, and that in this way he has taken upon himself all of our iniquities, our sins, our evil, making intercession for the transgressors.

Before we consider further this voluntary and innocent suffering of Christ, it is worth noting that although modern scholarship holds that this hymn of the Suffering Servant concludes at this point (Is 53.12), in the liturgical tradition of the Orthodox Church, the one time that this passage of Isaiah is read, at Vespers on Holy Friday, having read out all the passion narratives at Matins on the preceding evening, it continues and concludes with the following verse:

> Sing, O barren one, who did not bear; break forth into singing and cry aloud, you who have not been in travail! For the children of the

> desolate one will be more than the children of her that is married, says the LORD. (Is 54.1)

The Passion of Christ concludes with this joyful proclamation that the barren woman will give birth to children, for, after all, it is into the death of Christ that Christians are baptized as newly reborn children of God in their mother Church. It is by preaching the gospel of the crucified Lord that Paul is "in travail" with his converts, "until Christ be formed in you" (Gal 4.19), till they can say, as Paul had, that having been crucified with Christ "I no longer live, but Christ lives in me" (Gal 2.20)—for it is the Christians who are, individually and collectively, "the body of Christ" (1 Cor 12.27), all those who "by the one Spirit have been baptized into the one body" (1 Cor 12.13), calling upon God as "abba, Father" (Rom 8.15; Gal 4.6). As we will see, in Chapter Four, the Nativity of Christ is intimately connected to his Passion.

In this scriptural reflection on the Passion of Christ, the apostles, and the Church following after them, focused on the voluntary self-offering of Christ as an innocent victim. This is something that is affirmed in every celebration of the Divine Liturgy of St John Chrysostom, when the priest says, "in the night in which he was given up" and then adds, "or rather, gave himself up for the life of the world."[3] This movement from "given up" to "gave himself up" is really the turning point, at which a historical report becomes a theological reflection. Here theology proper begins. Christ was put to death, but in the light of God's vindication of the crucified Christ, we affirm that "he gave himself up for the life of the world."

If we think more deeply about this, we can begin to understand why, in the early Church, at least until the middle of the fourth century, the Crucifixion was not celebrated as a separate event from the Resurrection, as if they were two distinct actions or events: as if Christ died because he was human, but because he is also God he is able to get himself out of the grave. To put it in such terms would be very misleading and, in fact, a travesty. Such a separation is also evident in the caricature which claims that the Western church focuses on the darkness and sadness of Good Friday, while the Eastern church focuses on the light and joy of the Resurrection. Such a separation not only rends apart the inner unity of the celebration of Pascha, but also separates the humanity and divinity of Christ, as we shall see.

God's vindication of the crucified Jesus, not letting his holy one see corruption in the grave (Acts 2.25–32; Ps 16.10), does not remove from sight or sideline Jesus' death on the cross, but enables us to see this death as the voluntary self-offering of the innocent servant of the Lord, the conquering of death on the cross by one born of a virgin. In other words, the empty tomb is the confirmation of the victory wrought upon the Cross. Christ's exaltation in glory, the lifting-up spoken of by Isaiah, is precisely his exaltation on the Cross, as it is in the Gospel of John, to whose account we will shortly turn. As already noted, the first images of the Crucifixion depict the triumphant, living Lord upon the cross, with the Resurrection indicated, allusively, by the empty tomb with the stunned guards, and by the risen Christ greeting the myrrh-bearing women (as in the Rabbula Gospels, Plate 1). Only from the ninth century, a century or more after images of the Resurrection of Christ began to appear (about which we will have more to say), is Christ correspondingly depicted dead on the cross, although often, in Byzantine iconography, with the inscription on the cross now reading "The Lord of Glory."[4] Even when we have, as it were, refracted the pure white light of the Lord's Passion into a spectrum of colors, at the various services of Holy Week, and in the iconography of the Crucifixion and Resurrection, it is still this victory on the Cross that is celebrated at Pascha, during which we sing repeatedly that Christ has trampled down death *by death*. By his death, Christ conquers death—in no other way.

By his most human action, an action which expresses all the weakness and impotence of our created nature, Christ shows himself to be God. The profundity of this puts one at a loss for words. The transforming power of God is demonstrated through the death of Christ: not simply his death, by being put to death, but by his voluntary death, going to the Cross in obedience to his Father. This is "the mystery of the Lord," as Melito put it, that the angel already beheld in the blood of the lamb slain at the Exodus. This is also, in Paul's words, the "image of the invisible God" (Col 1.15). It is, moreover, in the one who has reconciled all to himself, "making peace by the blood of his Cross," that "all the fullness of God was pleased to dwell" (Col 1.19–20). As such, we cannot look anywhere else to understand who and what God is; there is no other means to come to know God. Those who stand in this tradition must follow the apostle Paul in refusing to know anything else apart from Christ and him crucified. Theology, as I suggested earlier, begins by reflecting on the Passion of Christ, contemplating there the transforming power of the eternal, timeless God.

THE GOD REVEALED THROUGH THE CROSS

This scriptural reflection on the Passion of Christ begun by the apostles and evangelists was continued, extended, and deepened in the work of subsequent theologians, shaping and informing every aspect of their theological vision. The centrality of the Passion of Christ as the locus of the revelation of the transformative power of God was particularly at issue in the debate against Eunomius in the latter part of the fourth century. Eunomius had accused St Basil the Great of being ashamed of the Cross, for having said, as Eunomius understood it, that it was merely a man who was crucified rather than a god.[5] After the death of St Basil, his brother, St Gregory of Nyssa, replied in full to Eunomius, claiming that it was, in fact, Eunomius who was ashamed of the Cross. St Gregory argued that the Passion of Christ is not "evidence of his weakness," as Eunomius took it, but evidence of "the surpassing act of power, by which this was possible," so that "it is necessary to honor the God revealed through the Cross just as the Father is honored."[6] So far is the Passion from being a mark of weakness, for St Gregory, that "the God revealed through the Cross" is not only honored, but honored equally with the Father.

This manifestation of the divine power of "the God revealed on the Cross" is, according to St Gregory, the central mystery of the apostolic proclamation:

> All who preach the Word point out the marvel of the mystery in this respect: that "God was manifested in the flesh" [1 Tim 3.16], that "the Word was made flesh" [Jn 1.14], that "the Light shone in the darkness" [Jn 1.5], "the Life tasted death" [Heb 2.9], and all such declarations which the heralds of the faith announce, whereby is increased the marvel of him who manifested the superabundance of his power by means external to his own nature.[7]

Scripture is clear that God is not seen by human beings, for divinity is not subject to human perception. In the case of the revelation of God in Jesus Christ, what is beheld is the transcendent power of divinity manifested precisely in the things external to the divine nature—in flesh, in darkness, and in death—for here we contemplate the transcendent and transforming power of God.

According to St Gregory, all these things proclaimed by the ministers of the Word not only persuade us to believe in the divinity of the crucified one, but also form the content for how we understand his divinity: it is the very expression of the Son's true divinity and equality, in honor and glory, with the Father. As Origen had put it, in the previous century, overturning our usual understanding of the "kenosis" hymn in Philippians 2:

> We must dare say that the goodness of Christ appeared greater and more divine and truly in accordance with the image of the Father when "he humbled himself and became obedient to death, even

> death on a cross," than if "he had considered being equal to God robbery," and had not been willing to become a servant for the salvation of the world.[8]

Christ's taking upon himself the role of a servant, voluntarily going to the Passion, does not diminish our perception of what we might otherwise have considered to be his divinity, but actually manifests his true divinity. The transcendent power of God is manifest in this world in flesh, in darkness and in death, as a servant. But this manifestation of divine power, in weakness, is simultaneously a transformation: Christ, in the form of a servant, shows us the image of God; darkness and death become light and life; and the flesh assumed by the Word, becomes flesh of the Word—and becomes Word. Or, as St Gregory put it, "even the body in which he underwent his Passion, by being mingled with the divine nature, was made by that commixture to be that which the assuming nature is."[9] Through the Passion, the body in which the Son suffered comes itself to share in the very divinity of God. Not that it is any the less human, but it is no longer subject to the density, opaqueness, and weight, together with the temporal and spatial limitations that characterize our own experience of our bodies: though Christ was once known after the flesh, he is known so no longer (cf. 2 Cor 5.16). The Passion remains as the locus for contemplating the transforming power of God, the "God revealed through the Cross."

THE COINCIDENCE OF OPPOSITES

The key scriptural passage for understanding the nature of this transformation, in the debate between St Gregory and Eunomius, is the statement of the apostle Peter in Acts 2.36, that "God has made him both Lord and Christ this Jesus whom you crucified." For Eunomius, these words meant that the crucified and exalted Lord Jesus Christ is straightforwardly a "creature," a "thing made." But for St Gregory, if he is exalted, he is so, as the apostle Peter said a few verses earlier, "by the Right Hand of God," the Right Hand of God which he is, for this is a title of Christ.[10] For St Gregory "the unspeakable economy of the mystery" is that "the Right Hand of God, who made all things that are . . . himself raised to his own height the man united to him, making him also, by the commixture, to be what he is by nature."[11] St Gregory continues, saying that when the apostle Peter says, in his "mystic discourse," that the crucified Jesus was "made Lord and Christ," this indicates that:

> the lowliness of the one crucified in weakness (and weakness, as we have heard from the Lord, indicates the flesh [Mt 26.41]), by virtue of its mingling with the infinite and boundless [nature] of the Good, remained no longer in its own measures and properties, but by the Right Hand of God was raised up together, and became Lord instead of servant, Christ the King instead of a subject, highest instead of lowly, God instead of man.[12]

Before the Passion, that is, we are obliged to recognize a different set of properties, those pertaining to the flesh in distinction to the Word. But this does not force us into separating the Word from the man, as two different subjects, because theology proper begins and ends with the contemplation of the crucified and exalted Christ—the one Lord Jesus Christ, the very Word of God.

Exalted, through the Passion, to become Lord and Christ, the lowliness of "the man" no longer remains "in its own measures and properties," but becomes that which the Right Hand of God himself is, identified with the one who exalts. In this sense, St Gregory affirms that it "is not as though one had suffered and another had been honored by exaltation"[13]: the one who exalts *is* the one who suffered. So, while, prior to the exaltation, the sufferings on the cross indicate nothing but the weakness of the flesh, prompting the disciples to abandon Christ, yet in the light of his exaltation, and the complete identity thus achieved, we can no longer make any such differentiation. "The unspeakable economy of the mystery" thus overturns all our usual categories: instead of a lowly, subjected servant, we now contemplate Christ the King, whose lordship is manifest in service; no longer man but God, or specifically, "the God revealed through the Cross."

We can, therefore, no longer contemplate the exalted "man" as in any way separate, distinguished by lowly properties, from the Right Hand of God. This identity achieved through the Passion means, in turn, that neither can we contemplate the one who brought all things into being as distinct from the crucified and exalted one. This coincidence of opposites is, for St Gregory, "the unsearchable riches of Christ," "the plan of the mystery hidden for ages in God who created all things" (Eph 3.8–9). When the apostle Paul speaks of its "breadth and length and height and depth" (Eph 3.18), St Gregory sees him as inscribing the figure of the cross into the very structure of the universe created by "the God revealed through the Cross."[14] The transcendent power of the eternal, timeless God, manifest in the Passion of Christ, is the same power that upholds all creation, so that the Cross is, indeed, the *axis mundi*, the still, eternal or timeless, axis around which the world rotates. It is likewise only in this way, "through the church," that the heavenly powers come to know "the manifold wisdom of God" (Eph 3.10). "It is truly through the church," St Gregory says in his *Commentary on the Song of Songs*, that the heavenly powers came to know "God's manifold wisdom, which marvelously works great wonders through opposites: how life came through death, righteousness through sin, blessing through curse, glory through disgrace, strength through weakness."[15] This coincidence of opposites that is the wisdom of God so delights Gregory that he devotes further lines to extolling it:

> This manifold form of wisdom, resulting from the plaiting together of opposites, is now clearly taught through the church: the Word

> becomes flesh, life is mixed with death, by his own bruises [Christ] heals our wounds, by the weakness of the Cross [he] overthrows the adversary's power . . . he is in death and life does not depart from him, he is mixed with slavery and remains in kingship.[16]

The union effected through the Passion, this coincidence of opposites, provides the proper basis for understanding what, in technical theological language, is referred to as the *communicatio idiomatum*, the exchange of properties. Contemplated by themselves, the properties of divinity and the flesh remain distinct: the Word is eternal while the flesh has come into being. These properties cannot simply be exchanged, to say, for example, that the flesh is eternal or the Word has come into being. Or, as St Gregory puts it, "It is not the human nature that raises up Lazarus, nor is it the power that cannot suffer that weeps for him when he lies in the grave; the tear is a property of the man, the life from the true Life."[17] But, as he continues, "because of the contact and union the [proper attributes] of each are common to both, the Lord receiving the blows of the servant and the servant receiving the lordly honor," so that the cross is properly said to be the Cross of the Lord of glory and Jesus is confessed as Lord to the glory of the Father.[18]

All of this means that it is not simply "in the flesh" that we contemplate the divine Word, the flesh which is perceived through the faculties by which we apprehend created reality. As we saw, the disciples did not fully understand who Christ is through their human contact with him. To ignore this point would ultimately reduce the Word of God to an object of physical perception, and theology to another human science. Rather, we contemplate the Word of God in the transformation wrought in the flesh and upon the flesh in the Passion of Christ, where we no longer see merely the suffering of the flesh, but contemplate the transforming power of the divine, forcing us to recognize the Lord as the one who suffered the blows and the servant as the Lord of glory, an identity brought into focus by the Cross. The focal point for the revelation of the Word of

God is not simply the Word's "becoming flesh," to be something other than what the Word eternally is, but rather it lies in the becoming Word of the flesh. Put in another way, it is in the apostolic preaching, the *kerygma*, narrated in the Gospels, that we "see" the Incarnate Word. As St Ignatius of Antioch put it at the turn of the second century, "Jesus Christ, being now in the Father, appears more clearly" than he was before.[19]

St Gregory concludes his presentation by resorting to a number of images in an attempt to illustrate this:

> At his death (which he brought about by his will . . . [Lk 23.46], [Jn 10.18]), this one, despising that which is shameful among men, because he is the Lord of glory, having concealed, as it were, the flame of life with his bodily nature, in the economy of his death kindled and inflamed it once more by the power of his own divinity, warming into life that which had died, and thus infusing with the infinity of his divine power that humble first-fruits of our nature, [he] made it also to be that which he himself was—the servile form, Lord; and the man, the Christ [born] of Mary; and him who was crucified through weakness, life and power; and making all that is piously contemplated in God the Word to be also in that which was assumed by the Word—so that these attributes no longer seem to be particularly in either by way of division, but that by its commixture with the divine, being made new in conformity with that which prevails, the perishable nature participates in the power of divinity. . . . This is our teaching, which . . . [proclaims] the union of the man to the divine, and which calls by the name of "making" the transformation of the mortal to the immortal, of the servant to the Lord, of sin to righteousness, of the curse to blessing, of the man to Christ.[20]

We do not contemplate the divine Word in the human, fleshly properties of Jesus Christ, as they were once perceived through the physical senses, but rather we encounter him in and through the Passion, for it is by the Passion that the identity of the crucified man and the Lord of glory is demonstrated. By the economy of his death, the flame of life is kindled and inflamed with the power of divinity, infusing the divine power into the humble first-fruits of our nature. In this way, as St Gregory puts it, the form of a servant is made Lord, and the man the Christ born of Mary, for as we will see in Chapter Four, the Nativity of Christ, as presented by Matthew and Luke, and celebrated in hymnography and depicted in iconography, is already based upon the proclamation of the gospel of the Crucified One. Furthermore, in this way the "division," by which each were separated according to their particular properties, no longer holds, for by commixture with the divine, "made new" in conformity with the prevailing divine power, man becomes God. There is, therefore, only one Christ, "made" Christ through his Passion, as a man, by which he simultaneously, as God, exalts himself. For St Gregory of Nyssa, the identity of the one Lord Christ hangs on the cross, known, no longer after the flesh, as one put to death, but in the Spirit, as one who gave himself to death, so conquering death.

THE GOSPEL OF JOHN

The transition we have observed, from perceiving the human Jesus to contemplating the one Lord Jesus Christ, the Word of God, can already be seen in the movement from the Synoptic Gospels to the Gospel of John. In both the Synoptics and the Gospel of John, the narrative culminates in the Passion. As Christ says, in the Gospel of John, "When you have lifted up [or "exalted"] the Son of man, then you will know that I AM."[21] That Christ is divine is known only from the perspective of the Cross, dying a human death, but doing so divinely, as God, giving himself up for the life of the world.

But in the Gospel of John, which from the early centuries has been regarded as the spiritual Gospel, written by the Theologian, Christ is presented quite differently both in the narrative that leads to the Passion and in the Passion itself. Indeed, although it is on the cross that Christ is "exalted," so that we might know that he is the Lord and that he might draw all people to himself (Jn 12.32), the actual day of the crucifixion is different: in the Synoptics, Christ holds the meal with his disciples on the day when the Passover lamb was sacrificed (Cf. Mt 26.17; Mk 14.12; Lk 22.7), while in the Gospel of John it is on this day that the crucifixion takes place (Jn 19.14), so that Christ is fully identified with the paschal lamb, an identity announced at the very beginning of the Gospel: "Behold the lamb of God who takes away the sin of the world" (Jn 1.29).

That Jesus Christ, the slain lamb, is the divine Word of God himself is a given for the Gospel of John from the beginning, and so the emphasis is on how he, as the divine Lord, voluntarily goes to the Cross. In the Gospel, Christ repeatedly speaks of himself as being "from above" (Jn 3.31, 8.23); he needs no transfiguration for us to behold his glory (Jn 1.14); and, although his soul is "troubled" as he approaches his Passion (Jn 12.27) and as he indicates that one of the disciples will betray him (Jn 13.21), Jesus does not struggle to reconcile himself to his Father's will, but instead offers a lengthy and profound meditation and prayer, beginning "Now is the Son of Man glorified and in him God is glorified" (Jn 13.31–17).

At the crucifixion itself, Christ is not abandoned in the Gospel of John. Instead we have the scene usually depicted in iconography, with his mother and the beloved disciple standing at the foot of the cross, together with his mother's sister, Mary the wife of Cleopas, and Mary Magdalene. On the cross Christ does not cry out, as in the other Gospels, "My God, My God, why have you forsaken me" (Mt 27.46; Mk 15.34; cf. Ps 22.1), but instead, after saying "I thirst," "to fulfill the scripture," receiving a sponge of vinegar (Jn 19.28–9; cf. Ps 69.21), Christ simply says, "It is finished" or "it is fulfilled," brought to completion or perfection (Jn 19.30): the work of God has been completed, and the Lord then rests from his works. The period of Christ's repose in the tomb, according to the hymnography for Holy Saturday, is the blessed Sabbath itself.

After saying "it is finished," Christ bows his head and, as it is usually translated, "gave up his spirit" (Jn 19.30). But as in the Gospel of John, and here alone, we have the mother and beloved disciple standing by the foot of the cross, we should perhaps understand it in the sense of Christ inclining his head towards his mother (as it is depicted in Byzantine iconography) and "handing over" or "traditioning the Spirit."[22] Perhaps now, we can understand a deeper sense to Christ's earlier words from the cross: "Woman behold your son," and to the disciple "Behold your mother" (Jn 19.26). While the beloved disciple is traditionally identified with the Evangelist himself, this is not actually an identification made by the Gospel; the only identification made here is that the one who stands by the cross of Christ and is not ashamed of him is the beloved disciple. Moreover, Christ does not say to his mother, "Woman behold another son for you in my place," but simply "behold your son." This bring us back to the point considered earlier: the faithful disciple who stands by the cross becomes identified with Christ—the son of Christ's own mother—putting on the identity of Christ, as Christians do in baptism, so that the barren one, the Church, now indeed has many children, as we saw Isaiah proclaiming. As John the Theologian describes the Passion, Christ ascends the cross and from the cross bestows the Spirit. The cycle of liturgical feasts in subsequent centuries follows the book of Acts to treat these actions more fully, by narrating and celebrating the Ascension and Pentecost separately, but, as with the distinction between the crucifixion and the exaltation considered earlier, their unity in the Passion of Christ should never be forgotten.

All that we have seen in this chapter is implied in the transition from "in the night in which he was given up" to "in the night in which he gave himself up"—the starting point for theology, a theology which does not simply speak about God in the abstract, nor satisfy itself with a historical report about events in the past, but which contemplates the transforming power of God revealed through the Cross, the eternal, timeless power that upholds all things, inviting and challenging us also to become transformed in its Word, putting on the identity of Christ.

NOTES

[1]Melito of Sardis *On Pascha* 32–33. Ed. and trans. S. G. Hall, OECT (Oxford: Clarendon Press, 1979); also trans. A. Stewart-Sykes (Crestwood, NY: St Vladimir's Seminary Press, 2001).

[2]Cf. A. D. Kartsonis, *Anastasis: The Making of an Image* (Princeton, NJ: Princeton University Press, 1986), 26; though she takes such images to indicate an inability to depict the dead Christ prior to a full articulation of the two natures of Christ following Chalcedon, ibid., 35–39.

[3]*Η ΘΕΙΑ ΛΕΙΤΟΥΡΓΙΑ—The Divine Liturgy* (Oxford: Oxford University Press, 1995), 32.

[4]Cf. J. R. Martin, "The Dead Christ on the Cross in Byzantine Art," in K. Weitzmann, ed., *Late Classical and Mediaeval Studies in Honor of Albert Mathias Friend* (Princeton: Princeton University Press, 1955), 189–96. That there was no depiction of the Resurrection prior to end of the seventh century, see Kartsonis, *Anastasis*, 28.

[5]St Gregory of Nyssa *Against Eunomius* 3.3.15–18. Ed. W. Jaeger, GNO 2 (Leiden: Brill, 2002 [1960]); Eng. trans. in NPNF, series 2, vol. 5, where this text of St Gregory is numbered as *Against Eunomius* 5 (pp. 172–81), and is differently subdivided into sections. As in what follows I only refer to this part of *Against Eunomius*, I will refer to this text simply as *Eunomius*, followed by the section number of GNO and that of NPNF in []: thus *Eunomius* 15–18 [2].

[6]*Eunomius* 34 [3]; 30 [3].

[7]*Eunomius* 35 [3].

[8]Origen *Commentary on John* 1.231. Ed. and French trans. C. Blanc, SC 120 (Paris: Cerf, 1966); Eng. trans. R. E. Heine, FC 80 (Washington, D.C.: Catholic University of America Press, 1989).

[9]St Gregory *Eunomius* 34 [3].

[10]Acts 2.33, though not as most modern translations render it: exalted "to the right hand of God."

[11]St Gregory *Eunomius* 44 [3].

[12]*Eunomius* 46 [3].

[13]*Eunomius* 42 [3].

[14]*Eunomius* 39–40 [4], citing Gal 6.14; 1 Cor 1.18; Eph 3.18–19.

[15]St Gregory of Nyssa *Commentary on the Song of Songs* 8. Ed. H. Langerbeck, GNO 6 (Leiden: Brill, 1986), 255; Eng. trans. C. McCambley (Brookline, MA: Hellenic College Press, 1987), 165.

[16]Ibid.

[17]St Gregory *Eunomius* 65 [5].

[18]*Eunomius* 66 [5].

[19]St Ignatius of Antioch *Letter to the Romans* 3.2. Letters of St Ignatius edited and trans. K. Lake, LCL Apostolic Fathers 1 (Cambridge, MA: Harvard University Press, 1985 [1912]).

[20]St Gregory *Eunomius* 68–69 [5].

[21]Jn 8.28, the RSV translates this, rather lamely, as "I am he."

[22]The same verb, "to hand over/tradition" is used here in Jn 19.30 as in the passages from the apostle Paul considered earlier in the chapter (i.e., 1 Cor 11.23, 15.3), and the Spirit is referred to simply with the article "the," not with the possessive pronoun "his."

CHAPTER TWO

Search the Scriptures

We began to explore the mystery of Christ in the last chapter by looking at how the disciples, as they are presented in the New Testament, came to understand the revelation of God in Christ. It was only after the Passion, in their encounter with the Risen Christ, that they finally knew him to be the Lord, as he opened the scriptures, showing that it was necessary for him to have undergone the Passion to enter into his glory, and broke bread with them (cf. Lk 24.25–32). Receiving the Spirit whom Christ had promised to send to bear witness to himself (Jn 15.26) and lead the disciples into all truth by taking what is his and declaring it to them (Jn 16.13–14), the disciples were then able to proclaim fully that "Jesus is Lord" (cf. 1 Cor 12.3), that is, the one spoken of in the scriptures.

PAST AND PRESENT CONFUSION

Before exploring further the mystery of Christ, we must take a step back, to consider why we took our starting point from the New Testament, and in so doing we will see in a little more detail how the apostles and evangelists "searched the scriptures," and that this is an ongoing task. We began with the events as they are described in the New Testament, and we are so familiar with this collection of texts that it is hard for us to imagine things in any other way. But it is a stubborn fact that for almost two centuries after Christ there was no such thing as a book called "The New Testament." Nor, for that matter, was the picture or pictures it presents the only version asserted: there were many other ways of explaining the work of God in Christ; many others claiming to be speaking on the authority of the Spirit or to be representing the true tradition; and, indeed, so many claimed to follow the apostle Paul that at the beginning of the third century Tertullian referred to him ironically as "the apostle of the heretics."[1] Some, such as Marcion, claimed that Paul had proclaimed a Christ who revealed a new god, a god of love and peace, distinct from the brutal and cruel god of the Old Testament. Others, such as Valentinus, and those usually designated today as "Gnostics," reused the imagery of the apostolic writings, in much the same way as the apostolic writings had reused the imagery of the Old Testament, in the production of their own allegedly inspired revelations, resulting in ever more complex mythologies describing all sorts of cosmic and pre-cosmic dramas. While yet others, such as Montanus, together with his prophetesses Maximilla and Priscilla, proclaimed a new dispensation and outpouring of the Spirit expressing itself in the form of a new and authoritative prophecy, greater enthusiasm, and more rigorous asceticism.

Such diverse claims, and there were more then (and even more now!), could not simply be answered by an appeal to the Spirit or to tradition, for they all claimed this for themselves. Nor could they be answered simply by an appeal to scripture, for what scripture is and how it is to be read are the very points at issue. Tertullian suggests that it is futile to argue on the basis of scriptures with those of other opinions, as such discussions will "produce no other effect than help to upset either the stomach or the brain"![2] If there was confusion about the proper approach to understanding the mystery of Christ in the first centuries following his Passion, there is even more confusion about such issues today, not only with modern variations of paths taken in the past—diverse forms of dispensationalism, new-age spiritualities, and charismatic figures—but also those resulting from our own modern presuppositions and predilections. In particular, now that we take for granted the existence of the New Testament, and have become accustomed to appealing to it, along with the Old Testament, as "inspired scripture," "the Word of God," and "the canon," our tendency is to treat scripture in a quite different manner than did the apostles and the early Church following them.

Having placed the source of authority in the inspired word of scripture or the inspired minds of its authors, we usually take our task to be the exposition of the inspired meaning residing within the text. So some today attempt to retrieve the original, pristine and pure, meaning of the authors of scripture by removing the obscuring sediment of later theological reflection. But to claim, on the basis of the New Testament, that something is what the apostle Paul, for instance, "really meant," is to forget that the very basis for that claim—the New Testament itself—is already the result of other, theological, factors; there were many claimants to Paul before there was a New Testament, and the portrait it sketches of the apostle was only one of many.

More frequent today, given our modern concern for history and historical truth, are investigations undertaken in the form of an archaeological excavation, reconstructing "what really happened" by applying our modern criteria of historical plausibility. The most notorious example of this is the "Jesus Seminar" with its attempt to determine what words or actions attributed to Jesus can reliably be asserted to be historically authentic, and then to use this as the basis for criticizing or repristinating Christianity. One could similarly point to those magazines and television programs that, with tedious repetitiveness, publish issues and broadcast "documentaries" to coincide with Christmas and Easter, claiming to investigate "what really happened." On the basis of such reconstructions, and using other witnesses excluded from the New Testament, it is sometimes asserted that the message brought by Jesus was one of liberation and equality (rather reassuringly modern sentiments), a message which others attempted to terminate by putting him to death, and that the proclamation of the crucified Lord continues this repressive movement for the sake of maintaining the patriarchal status quo.

In striking contrast with this attempt to establish a single narrative of "what really happened," early Christians were prepared to accept four different versions of what happened. Although, in the mid-second century, Tatian did attempt to produce a "Gospel Harmony" (his *Diatessaron*), smoothing out the differences between the apostolic accounts in a narrative of his own construction, the fourfold account was accepted in canonical scripture. Other than the fact that Jesus was crucified (a public event, after all, and the starting point or catalyst for the apostolic proclamation), the different accounts in the four Gospels contain irresolvable discrepancies, from the most obvious, such as the timing of the cleansing of the temple (at the beginning of Christ's ministry in John, towards the end in the Synoptics), the timing of the crucifixion (on the day when the Passover lamb was sacrificed in John, but on the following day in the Synoptics), the words of Christ from the cross, and the resurrectional appearances, to almost insignificant details, such as whether the cock crowed once (as in Matthew, Luke, and John) or twice (in Mark). Some early Christians were even prepared to see in these discrepancies divinely placed "stumbling blocks" to direct our attention to the higher level of theological reflection that the Gospels present, rather than the mere letter or the mere history; for them, the four Gospels are already interpretations of the person and work of Jesus Christ, made from the perspective of the Passion and expounded with reference to the scriptures—the Law, the Psalms, and the Prophets.

Another aspect of the confusion that exists around these issues is the relationship between scripture and tradition. The problem here seems to arise from treating scripture and tradition as if they were equivalent but distinct sources of authority and information. Some in the second century, especially the Gnostics according to St Irenaeus, made the claim, repeated many times thereafter, that it is impossible to understand scripture without knowing tradition, that tradition supplied information handed down by the apostles apart from their writings, and that this alone enabled one to know the truth. The Reformation, of course, asserted that scripture alone is sufficient for a knowledge of the truth. Many voices since have argued in reaction that scripture is a part of tradition, on the grounds that scripture was written within the Church and that the Church has determined which books are to count as scripture.

Each of these positions, however, raises difficulties. If, on the one hand, authority is located solely in scripture, as itself the "Word of God" and the "canon" (understood in the sense of a "list" of authoritative books), then accounting for that list of books becomes problematic: why these texts and not others? Why not include the *Gospel of Thomas* or any of the other numerous texts that claim apostolic authorship? If, on the other hand, scripture is placed within tradition, then on what basis does one distinguish between what is true and valuable in tradition and what is not, for as St Cyprian put it, "Custom without truth is but the antiquity of error";[3] one is left claiming that some things are "Holy Tradition" while others are only "traditions," yet not providing a criterion by which this distinction is made.

In large measure, the confusion that exists today regarding the basis of Christian faith results from taking for granted the existence of the New Testament, and then turning to it for the primary testimony to Christ and considering its allusions to the Old Testament as a secondary layer, added only subsequently to make some rather arbitrary connections. Yet, as we saw in the previous chapter, even within the New Testament, it is only when the crucified and exalted Christ opened the scriptures to show how they spoke of him, that the disciples began to understand that he is the Lord. The conversation between the apostle Philip and the Ethiopian eunuch also demonstrates this, and brings to light a further difference between our modern quest for meaning and the manner in which the early Christians approached scripture. When Philip found the eunuch sitting in his chariot reading the hymn of the Suffering Servant from the prophet Isaiah, the eunuch's question was not the one that we would ask today—"What is the meaning of this passage?"—as if the "meaning" were located in the text itself, and so in the past, and our task is simply to uncover it, what the text "meant," and then perhaps try to find "meaning" for ourselves in the present by some kind of analogy. Instead, the eunuch asked, "About whom does the prophet say this, about himself or about some one else?" (Acts 8.34). "Meaning" resides in the person of whom the text speaks, and our task is to come to know this person by understanding how the text speaks of him.

This fundamental point is made by Christ himself, when he says, "You search the scriptures, because you think that in them you have eternal life, yet it is they that witness to me" (Jn 5.39). To emphasize the point, he says a few verses later, "If you believed Moses, you would believe me, for he wrote of me" (Jn 5.46). Moses certainly wrote in the past, but the "meaning" of his words is neither as a straightforward description of historical events in the past nor as having "meant" something that we can now retrieve by reconstructing the past. Rather the "meaning" of his words, once again, lies in how he speaks of the Lord Jesus Christ. Given this locus of the "meaning" of scripture, we can now understand why for the authors of the writings of the New Testament, and those whose work resulted in these writings being collected together, the expression "the Word of God" did not refer to scripture, as it is often assumed today, but to Jesus Christ himself and the gospel proclaiming him, the crucified and exalted one, as Lord.

Another term which is often used incorrectly today is "canon." This term simply means a guideline, a rule or straight line by which one can determine the straightness of other lines. It is, therefore, something appealed to as a criterion to determine the correctness or accuracy of whatever is being assessed. In modern times (since 1768), the term has acquired a second meaning, that of "list," in particular, the list of authoritative books.[4] But in antiquity, the term was not used in this way, and indeed it could not have been. When, today, "the canon of scripture" is spoken of, there is a sleight of hand at work: on the one hand, the expression refers to the list of books contained in scripture, but on the other hand, by speaking of this list as "canon," a regulative function is attributed to it. There have, therefore, been innumerable studies in recent centuries, attempting to determine precisely which books came to be counted as scripture in different places and at different times. Such works usually note that the term "canon" primarily meant "rule," yet presuppose that it is the "list" that is most important, and then devote their attention to such "lists" while ignoring what early Christians in fact said about the "canon" or "rule."

In fact, there was remarkably little concern in antiquity to catalog the authentic or genuine books of scripture. In part this was because they soon became commonly accepted; collections of the letters of Paul seem to have been in existence towards the end of the first century, and a fourfold Gospel collection soon after.[5] The limits of such collections were not universally agreed upon, and there were indeed occasional discussions about what was to count as sacred scripture. These were, however, only sporadic; no council was called to determine the issue. A couple of the smaller councils did produce lists as part of their deliberations, and various bishops issued statements with the same purpose, but these invariably disagree with one another.[6]

The main concern of early Christians was not to determine the exact boundaries of sacred scripture; this only acquires the importance it has today if we assume that meaning and authority reside within the text itself. But given what we have seen, that "meaning" resides in the person of Christ, who is himself the truth (Jn 14.6), it is not surprising that there was instead a continual debate, from the beginning, about the person and work of Christ—how he relates to God and to us, how he is made known, through the Spirit, and how it is that scripture speaks of all this. The "pattern of sound words," which Timothy heard from the apostle Paul and which the apostle urged him to follow (2 Tim 1.13), by the end of the second century came to be expressed as a "canon of truth," a creed-like statement of faith in one God, one Lord Jesus Christ, and one Holy Spirit.

THE CANON AND TRADITION OF THE GOSPEL ACCORDING TO SCRIPTURE

In order, then, to bring clarity to how we explore the mystery of Christ, as we began to do in the previous chapter on the basis of the New Testament, we need to consider the theological framework in which this collection of texts was brought together, a framework composed of scripture, together with a canon of truth, and an appeal to apostolic tradition and apostolic succession. This framework was established, at the end of the second century, by St Irenaeus of Lyons, in a manner which thereafter became the milieu or atmosphere of Orthodox or Catholic Christianity, the Christianity of what the pagan critic Celsus called "the Great Church." The particular genius of St Irenaeus is his demonstration that the coherence and interrelationship of these four elements—scripture (the "Old Testament," but now also, in this framework, the "New Testament"), the canon or rule of truth, apostolic tradition, and apostolic succession—lies in nothing other than the proclamation of the crucified and exalted Christ "in accordance with scripture," in other words, with the way in which the gospel had been preached from the beginning.

This is not to claim that "orthodoxy" preceded "heresy," and that all we need to do is to preserve intact an inert or static body of knowledge or customs. It would be a mistake to look to the past in an attempt to find an original and pristine Christianity, whether that of the Jerusalem community described in the book of Acts, the early Christianity of Eusebius' *Ecclesiastical History*, or the later eras of imperial Christianity, whether Western or Eastern. Indeed, the earliest Christian texts that we have, the letters of the apostle Paul, are already written in response to errors arising in the Christian communities. The truth of Christianity is not protological, but rather eschatological, residing in Christ whose return Christians still await; even in the Gospels, he is described as "the coming one" (cf. Mt 11:3; 21:9; 23:39). The faith delivered ("traditioned") to the saints once for all (Jude 3) is preserved in an orientation, a particular manner of approaching the mystery of Christ, which St Irenaeus encapsulates in terms of the mutuality of scripture, canon, tradition, and succession, all bearing witness to Christ and his gospel.

In the last chapter, we saw how images from the Old Testament were used to expound the mystery of Christ. The process of re-employing images to understand and explain the present in terms of the scriptures, and so in turn the scriptures as anticipating the present, was at work throughout the Old Testament, as, for instance, when Noah is presented, after the flood, being blessed to preside over a renewed world, using the vocabulary and imagery of the opening chapters in Genesis (cf. Gen 9.1–7, 1.26–31). With the proclamation of the crucified and exalted Lord, however, this process stops and, in a sense, begins anew. As all things are made new in Christ (Rev 21.5), even scripture itself, the Old Testament, must now be read in a new manner. However it was that the disciples of Christ had previously read scripture, and we know that there were many and diverse ways of reading scripture—from the Pharisees to the Dead Sea Covenanters to the Hellenized Philo—they were not expecting God to reveal himself in this way, in an exalted, crucified Messiah.

What has happened in Christ is the definitive, "once for all," work of God, and this informs or shapes how followers of Christ read scripture thereafter, seeking to understand him. St Irenaeus, in a lengthy but beautiful passage, sets this out, and more, with great clarity:

> If anyone, therefore, reads the scriptures this way, he will find in them the Word concerning Christ, and a foreshadowing of the new calling. For Christ is the "treasure which was hidden in the field" [Mt 13.44], that is, in this world—for "the field is the world" [Mt 13.38]—[a treasure] hidden in the scriptures, for he was indicated by means of types and parables, which could not be understood by human beings prior to the consummation of those things which had been predicted, that is, the advent of the Lord. And therefore it was said to Daniel the prophet, "Shut up the words, and seal the book, until

> the time of the consummation, until many learn and knowledge abounds. For, when the dispersion shall be accomplished, they shall know all these things" [Dan 12.4, 7]. And Jeremiah also says, "In the last days they shall understand these things" [Jer 23.20]. For every prophecy, before its fulfillment, is nothing but an enigma and ambiguity to human beings; but when the time has arrived, and the prediction has come to pass, then it has an exact exposition [*exegesis*]. And for this reason, when at this present time the Law is read by the Jews, it is like a myth, for they do not possess the explanation [*exegesis*] of all things which pertain to the human advent of the Son of God; but when it is read by Christians, it is a treasure, hid in a field, but brought to light by the Cross of Christ, and explained, both enriching the understanding of humans, and showing forth the wisdom of God, and making known his dispensations with regard to human beings, and prefiguring the kingdom of Christ, and preaching in anticipation the good news of the inheritance of the holy Jerusalem, and proclaiming beforehand that the one who loves God shall advance so far as even to see God, and hear his Word, and be glorified, from hearing his speech, to such an extent, that others will not be able to behold his glorious countenance [cf. 2 Cor 3.7], as was said by Daniel, "Those who understand shall shine as the brightness of the firmament, and many of the righteous as the stars for ever and ever" [Dan 12.3]. In this manner, then, I have shown it to be, if anyone read the scriptures.[7]

St Irenaeus brings together, in a quite extraordinary manner, the discovery of Christ in and through the scriptures (which here refers to the Old Testament) and the transfiguration of the one encountering Christ in this manner, such that they become like Moses as he descended the mountain after his encounter with God.

The effect of such exegesis upon the disciple reading scripture in this way will be treated in later chapters. For now, we need to consider this discipline of reading itself. The image given by Christ, of treasure hidden in the field or the world, is used by St Irenaeus to refer to Christ himself: he is the treasure hidden in scripture, and so scripture, in turn, is the treasury in which we find him. Scripture is a "thesaurus" (the Greek word for "treasury"), a compendium of the words and images with which we, as it were, articulate the mystery of Christ, the Christ proclaimed "in accordance with the scriptures." Particularly important in this manner of reading scripture, which should be no surprise by now, is that St Irenaeus is emphatic that it operates from the perspective of the Cross. Those who read scripture without the explanation of the treasure that it contains, the gospel it anticipates, see in scripture only myths and fables. It is through the Cross that light is shed upon the scriptures, removing the veil that lay over Moses himself and now lies upon those who read Moses without a knowledge of Christ, so revealing the glory that Moses concealed with the veil, "the light of the gospel of the glory of Christ," making known "the knowledge of the glory of God in the face of Christ," and inviting others to share in this glory (cf. 2 Cor 3.7–4.6).

HYPOTHESIS AND CANON

For St Irenaeus it is quite clearly not scripture itself that is being exegeted, at least not in the sense of modern historical-critical "exegesis" in its attempt to understand the "original meaning" of an ancient text, but rather Christ who is being expounded through the medium of scripture, drawing upon its treasury of images and words. Seen in this way, the whole of scripture (again, the Old Testament) is understood as speaking of the crucified and exalted Christ and, as such, acquires a coherence and unity which it did not have, or at least was not known to have, prior to the proclamation of the gospel.

To describe this, St Irenaeus uses the image of a mosaic, with the treasury that is scripture providing the various gem stones used to portray the

Lord and, in so doing, begins to introduce the idea of canon, tradition, and succession. After describing some of the Gnostic myths, St Irenaeus criticizes their use of scripture in a lengthy, but important, passage:

> Such is their hypothesis which neither the prophets preached, nor the Lord taught, nor the apostles handed down. They boast rather loudly of knowing more about it than others do, citing it from unwritten [or: unscriptural] sources; and as people would say, they attempt to braid ropes of sand. They try to adapt to their own sayings in a manner worthy of credence, either the Lord's parables or the prophets sayings, or the apostles' words, so that their fabrication might not appear to be without witness. They disregard the order and the connection of the scriptures and, as much as in them lies, they disjoint the members of the truth. They transfer passages and rearrange them; and, making one thing out of another, they deceive many by the badly composed fantasy of the Lord's words that they adapt. By way of illustration, suppose someone would take the beautiful image of a king, carefully made out of precious stones by a skilful artist, and would destroy the features of the man on it and change it around and rearrange the jewels, and make the form of a dog or of a fox out of them, and that rather a bad piece of work. Suppose he would then say with determination that this is the beautiful image of the king that the skilful artist had made, and at the same time pointing to the jewels which had been beautifully fitted together by the first artist into the image of the king, but which had been badly changed by the second into the form of a dog. And suppose he would through this fanciful arrangement of the jewels deceive the inexperienced who had no idea of what the king's picture looked like, and would persuade them that this base picture of a fox is that beautiful image of the king. In the same way these people patch together old women's fables, and then pluck words and sayings and parables from here and there and wish to adapt these words of God to their myths.[8]

His opponents have a "hypothesis" which does not derive from the Lord or the apostles but is rather their own fabrication, which they then explicate with words from the scriptures, adapting the words of God to their own myths, in an attempt to endow it with persuasive plausibility. As such, they "disregard the order and the connection of the scriptures and "disjoint the members of the truth." They are, in his vivid image, like someone taking a mosaic of a king and rearranging the stones to make a picture of a dog or a fox, claiming that this is the original, true image.

St Irenaeus follows this with a more literary example, describing how some people take diverse lines from the work of Homer and then rearrange them to produce a Homeric-sounding poem, a cento, which tells a tale not found in Homer: those who have only a passing knowledge of Homer are likely to be deceived; but those who are well versed in his poetry will be able to identify the lines and restore them to their proper context.

The terms which St Irenaeus uses are all technical terms in Hellenistic literary theory and philosophy. The term "fabrication" describes stories that are not true but seem to be so, and "myth" refers to stories that are manifestly untrue. So, according to Irenaeus, the Gnostics start with their own fantastic myths and then cloak them with the language of scripture. The term "hypothesis" had a variety of meanings. In a literary context, it meant the plot or outline of a drama or epic: that which the poet posits as the outline for his subsequent creative work. It is not derived from reasoning, but presupposed, providing a skeleton, as it were, which is enfleshed by the words of the poet exercising his talent. As St Irenaeus put it, although the myths of his opponents use the words and phrases from scripture, they have adapted them to a different hypothesis, and so have created their own fabrication.

In the other arts similarly, the hypothesis, as that which is posited, the presupposition, facilitates both action and inquiry, and ultimately knowledge itself. Hypotheses are, as Aristotle put it, the starting points or first principles of demonstrations.[9] For instance, the goal of health is the hypothesis for a doctor, who then deliberates on how it is to be attained, just as mathematicians hypothesize certain axioms and then proceed with their demonstrations. Such hypotheses are tentative; if the goal proves to be unattainable or if the conclusions derived from the supposition turn out to be manifestly false, then the hypothesis in question must be rejected. So, according to St Irenaeus, his opponents have based their exegesis of scripture upon their own "hypothesis," rather than that foretold by the prophets, taught by Christ, and delivered ("traditioned") by the apostles.

At least since the time of Plato, the aim of philosophy has been to discover the ultimate, nonhypothetical first principle. But even here, as Aristotle conceded, it is impossible to demand demonstrations of the first principle itself; if it could be proved, it would necessarily be dependent upon something prior to it, and so one would be led into an infinite regress.[10] This means, as Clement of Alexandria points out, that the search for the first principle of any demonstration ends up with indemonstrable faith.[11] What is accepted as the first principle of knowledge cannot itself be demonstrated, and so is accepted on faith. For Christian faith, according to Clement, it is the Lord who speaks in scripture, the Word of God himself, that is the first principle of all knowledge.[12] The voice of the Lord, speaking throughout scripture, is the first principle, the (nonhypothetical) hypothesis of all demonstrations from scripture, by which Christians are led to the knowledge of the truth.

This first principle accepted by faith as that which is given—the Lord himself who is the truth (Jn 14.6)—is not only the starting point for subsequent demonstrations, but is also used to evaluate other claims to truth, finding expression as a "canon," the next technical term that Irenaeus introduces. After criticizing the Gnostics for their distortion of scripture, he continues:

> Anyone who keeps unswervingly in himself the canon of truth received through baptism will recognize the names and sayings and

> parables from the scriptures, but this blasphemous hypothesis of theirs he will not recognize. For if he recognizes the jewels, he will not accept the fox for the image of the king. He will restore each one of the passages to its proper order and, having fit it into the body of the truth, he will lay bare their fabrication and show that it is without support.[13]

Originally the term "canon" simply meant a straight line, a rule by which other lines could be judged: "By that which is straight, we discern both the straight and the crooked; for the carpenter's rule (*canon*) is the test of both, but the crooked tests neither itself nor the straight."[14] Without a canon or criterion, knowledge is not possible, for all inquiry will be drawn helplessly into an endless regression. So, in the face of radical Skepticism, it became almost obligatory in the Hellenistic period to begin any systematic presentation of philosophy with an account of "the criterion." In the same way in which Hellenistic philosophers argued against the infinite regression of the Skeptics by appealing to a canon or criterion of truth, St Irenaeus appealed to the canon of truth to counter the constantly mutating Gnostic mythology.

For St Irenaeus, the faith received in baptism (in the name of Father, Son, and Holy Spirit) acts as a canon, by reference to which scripture can be understood properly, so that the image of Christ can be contemplated. Irenaeus follows this by outlining what has been received from the apostles:

> The faith in one God the Father Almighty, Creator of heaven and earth and all the seas and all things that are in them;
>
> and in one Jesus Christ, the Son of God, who was enfleshed for our salvation;
>
> and in the Holy Spirit, who through the prophets preached the economies—the coming, the birth from a Virgin, the passion, the resurrection from the dead, and the bodily ascension into heaven of

> the beloved Son, Christ Jesus our Lord, and his coming from heaven in the glory of the Father to recapitulate all things, and to raise up all flesh of the whole human race, in order that to Christ Jesus our Lord and God, Savior and King, according to the invisible Father's good pleasure, "every knee should bow [of those] in heaven and on earth and under the earth, and every tongue confess" him [Phil 2.10–11], and that he would exercise just judgment towards all: and that, on the one hand, he would send into eternal fire the spiritual forces of wickedness, and the angels who transgressed and became rebels, and the godless, wicked, lawless, and blasphemous people; but, on the other hand, by bestowing life on the righteous and holy and those who kept his commandments and who have persevered in his love—both those who did so from the beginning and those who did so after repentance—he would bestow on them as a grace the gift of incorruption and clothe them with everlasting glory.[15]

This description is clearly structured upon the same three central articles of belief found in the baptismal interrogations from the earliest times, going back to the baptismal command of Christ himself (Mt 28.19) and which also shape the later creeds, such as those of the Councils of Nicaea (AD 325) and Constantinople (AD 381). A noteworthy difference between this canon of truth given by St Irenaeus and the later creeds is the fact that all the actions of Christ recounted in the Gospels are presented under the third article, the Holy Spirit. In the later creeds, these events are placed under the second article, leaving unspecified what the Spirit "spoke through the prophets." For St Irenaeus, on the other hand, the primary reference for the person and work of Christ is the (Old Testament) scripture, read according to the Spirit given by the crucified and risen Christ.

So, for St Irenaeus, the canon of truth does not simply give fixed, and abstract, statements of Christian doctrine to be used as building blocks, as it were, for metaphysical systems, but expresses the correct hypothesis of scripture itself, the presupposition by which one can see in scripture the picture of a king, Christ, rather than a dog or fox. One must, for instance, hold that the God of the Law, the Psalms, and the Prophets is indeed the Father of Jesus Christ—the first article of any canon or creed—if one is not to end up with a falsified picture. As a canon, it enables the believer to demonstrate the incongruous and extraneous nature of the Gnostic hypotheses. By means of the same canon of truth, the various passages, the "members of truth," can be returned to their rightful place within "the body of truth," scripture, so that it again speaks of Christ, while exposing the Gnostic fabrications for what they are.[16]

The canon of truth thus expresses or crystallizes the presupposition that is the apostolic Christ himself, the one who is "according to the scripture," and, in reverse, the subject of scripture throughout, being spoken of by the Spirit through the prophets, so revealing the one God and Father. The canon of truth is thus inextricably connected, for Irenaeus, with "the order and the connection of the scriptures," for it presents the one Father who has made himself known through the one Son by the Holy Spirit speaking through the prophets, that is, through the scriptures—the Law, the Psalms, and the Prophets.

Put in another way, the canon of truth is the formal structure of the harmony of scripture, read as speaking of the Christ revealed in the apostolic preaching "in accordance with the scripture." Clement of Alexandria provides a concise definition of the canon in such terms when he states:

> The ecclesiastical canon is the concord and harmony of the law and the prophets in the covenant delivered at the coming of the Lord.[17]

The hypothesis, or the presupposition, of the Christian faith—the crucified and risen Lord himself—reveals the symphony of the scriptures when he opens the books to show how they all speak of himself, the one presented by the apostles "in accordance with the scripture." The pattern of this harmony is expressed in the canon of truth, enabling the demonstrations from scripture to describe, accurately, the portrait of a king, Christ. The canon of truth thus provides the framework for the encounter with the Christ proclaimed by the apostles, an encounter which takes place through the engagement with the matrix of imagery provided by the scriptures.

CANONICAL, INSPIRED SCRIPTURE

Seen in this way, we can now perhaps understand the theological (if not historical, for this is now lost to us, if it were ever explicit) rationale which lay behind the collection of texts that we know as the New Testament. As already noted, it seems that letters of the apostle Paul were already being gathered into collections by the end of the first century, and a four-fold Gospel collection followed soon thereafter. There are plenty of allusions to the writings that came to be collected into the New Testament, by writers such as St Ignatius at the beginning of the second century and others subsequently, but this is only to be expected, since they were concerned with the same proclamation as the apostles. It is only with St Irenaeus at the end of the second century, however, that these writings were extensively and consistently used as sacred scripture and that we have what is recognizably a New Testament. For St Irenaeus, the fourfold Gospel was already part of tradition, and he defends it in a manner which is clearly "after the fact"—there can be no more or less than four Gospels as there are four zones in the world and four principal winds.[18]

However, given what we have seen of the canon of truth, it seems likely that the theological rationale for these Gospels alone being held as canonical is that is that each of the Gospels of Matthew, Mark, Luke, and John, are centered upon the Passion of Christ and are proclaimed using the treasury of scripture, the Old Testament. The very "beginning of the Gospel of Jesus Christ" in Mark is illustrated by the citation of a passage from Isaiah (Mk 1:1–3; Mal 3:1; Is 40:3). In Matthew, the same engagement with scripture is found throughout, in terms of prophecy-fulfillment structuring the narrative. In Luke it appears as the hermeneutic, the principle of interpretation, taught by the risen Christ, thereby enlightening his disciples: "Beginning with Moses and all the prophets, he interpreted to them in all the scriptures the things concerning himself" (Lk 24:27, cf. Lk 24:44–49). This literary enlightening of the disciples is paralleled in John when Christ breathes on his disciples the Holy Spirit, the one he had promised, who would remind them of all things concerning Christ, leading them into all truth (cf. Jn 20:22; 14:26); Word and Spirit can never be separated, and both are at work in the task of interpretation. It is also in John where the relationship between the scriptures and Christ is stated most emphatically, by Christ himself: "If you believed Moses, you would believe me, for he wrote of me" (Jn 5:46).

In contrast, this engagement with scripture, read in the light of the apostolic proclamation of the crucified Lord, is glaringly absent from noncanonical works such as the *Gospel of Thomas* or has taken a very different turn in, for instance, the Valentinian *Gospel of Truth*, where the apostolic writings are refashioned, on the basis of a different hypothesis, to produce a different fabrication.[19] They might preserve authentic historical information, although to claim that their "truth" resides in this would be to substitute a criterion other than the canon of truth, and to subject Christ, the truth himself, to our own measures for determining what is true. Such measures are, in fact, nothing more than the persuasiveness of historical plausibility, and change with the changing sensibilities of the age, resulting in the multitude of books claiming to present the "real Jesus" that are found weighing down shelves at many bookstores. More importantly, in the *Gospel of Truth*, and other similar works, the engagement with scripture has a very different hypothesis or starting point, and in the *Gospel of Thomas*, there is no engagement with scripture at all, nor is there a Passion.

With this determination of what constitutes canonical scripture, we can also begin to understand how these works were regarded as "inspired." For early Christians, this inspiration was not thought to reside solely within the text of scripture or in the mind of the inspired prophet as he uttered or wrote his words. If it were this, our task would then be to discern the "original meaning" of the text or the "mind of the author," ideas which are distinctively modern and which have been abandoned by recent literary theory.[20] As it is only when Christ himself opens the scriptures, to show how they all speak of him and his Passion, that the inspired meaning of the scriptures is brought to light, the inspiration of the scriptures cannot be separated from the opening of the sealed book by the slain Lamb (Rev 5). This, in turn, requires an "inspired" reading of the scriptures, guided by the same Spirit of Christ, the one by whom Christ spoke through Moses, David, Isaiah, and others.

APOSTOLIC TRADITION AND SUCCESSION

As St Irenaeus continues his discussion about the canon of truth, he brings in two further elements of the framework of the Christianity of the Great Church. The key elements of the faith delivered by the apostles are crystallized in the canon of truth, which expresses the basic elements of the one gospel, maintained and preached in the Church, in an ever-changing context. The continually changing context in which the same unchanging gospel is preached makes it necessary that different aspects or facets of the same gospel be drawn out to address contemporary challenges. However, while the context continually changes, the content of that tradition does not—it is the same gospel. So, after stating the canon of truth quoted earlier, St Irenaeus continues:

> The Church . . . though disseminated throughout the world, carefully guards this preaching and this faith, which she has received, as if she

> dwelt in one house. She likewise believes these things as if she had but one soul and one and the same heart; she preaches, teaches and hands them down harmoniously, as if she possessed one mouth. For though the languages of the world are dissimilar, nevertheless the meaning [or force] of tradition is one and the same. To explain, the churches which have been founded in Germany do not believe or hand down anything else; neither do those founded in Spain or Gaul or Libya or in the central regions of the world. But just as the sun, God's creation, is one and the same throughout the world, so too, the light, the preaching of the truth, shines everywhere and enlightens all men who wish to come to a knowledge of the truth. Neither will any of those who preside in the churches, though exceedingly eloquent, say anything else (for no one is above the Master); nor will a poor speaker subtract from the tradition. For, since the faith is one and the same, neither he who can discourse at length about it adds to it, nor he who can say only a little subtracts from it.[21]

As the faith is the same, those who can speak endlessly about it do not add to it, any more than those who are poor speakers detract from it, for the meaning or the content of tradition is one and the same. While Christians are called to live in this tradition, and to give it ever new expression, the tradition itself does not "grow" or "develop" into something else.[22] The Church is to guard carefully this preaching and this faith, which she has received and which she is to preach, teach, and hand down harmoniously.

St Irenaeus takes up his examination of the relation between scripture and tradition in the opening five chapters of the third book of his work, *Against the Heresies.* This time his concern is to counter the Gnostic claims to possess secret, oral traditions. He begins by affirming categorically that the revelation of God is mediated through the apostles. It is not enough to see the "Jesus of history" to see God, nor to imagine God as a partner with whom one can dialogue directly, by-passing his own

Word. Rather the locus of revelation, and the medium for our relationship with God, is precisely in the apostolic preaching of him, the gospel which, as we have seen, stands in an interpretative engagement with scripture. The role of the apostles in delivering the gospel is definitive. As St Irenaeus opens his first chapter:

> We have learned from no others the plan of our salvation than from those through whom the gospel has come down to us, which they did at one time proclaim in public, and at a later period, by the will of God, handed down (*tradiderunt*) to us in the scriptures, to be the ground and pillar of our faith. . . . These have all declared to us that there is one God, Creator of heaven and earth, announced by the Law and Prophets; and one Christ the Son of God.[23]

That is, for St Irenaeus, both the true apostolic tradition maintained by the churches, and the apostolic writings themselves, derive from the same apostles and have one and the same content, the gospel, which is itself "in accordance with the scriptures."

This allows St Irenaeus to reject his opponents' appeal to a tradition that has been handed down in secret and by word of mouth, without which, they claim, scripture cannot be understood, because, as he points out, what the apostles taught in public is identical to what they wrote down. Far from preserving an authentic tradition, Marcion and Valentinus have distorted the canon of truth and merely preached themselves.[24] St Irenaeus, on the other hand, does appeal to tradition and even imagines a scenario in which the apostles left nothing behind in writing, so that only the oral tradition exists, but in these cases the tradition he appeals to is again identical with what is written down by the apostles.[25] St Irenaeus also appeals to the publicly visible continuity of this tradition, in the successions of the bishops or presbyters (the terms were still used interchangeably by him) of the various churches, most importantly, but not exclusively, that of Rome, by which "the ecclesiastical tradition from the apostles and the preaching of the truth have come down to us."[26] St Irenaeus' appeal to tradition and succession is thus fundamentally different to that of his opponents. While they appealed to tradition precisely for that which was not in scripture, or for principles which would legitimize their interpretation of scripture, St Irenaeus, in his appeal, was not appealing to anything that was not also in scripture. In this way, he can appeal to tradition to establish his case and at the same time maintain that scripture cannot be understood except on the basis of scripture itself, using its own hypothesis and canon.[27]

Having established that the apostolic tradition does now exist in the Church, preserved through the successions of the presbyters who have held intact the true preaching, St Irenaeus then turns to "the demonstration from the scriptures of the apostles who wrote the gospel, in which they recorded the doctrine regarding God, pointing out that our Lord Jesus Christ is the truth, and that there is no lie in Him."[28] Scripture, as written, is fixed, and though the tradition maintained by the succession of presbyters is similarly fixed in principle, in practice it is much less secure, and, in any case, it can never be, for St Irenaeus, a point of reference apart from scripture. The doctrine concerning God, and the truth that is Christ, is found in the exposition of the scriptures as interpreted by the apostles, who alone proclaimed the gospel, handing it down in both scripture and tradition. In this way, the apostolic writings are recognized as belonging to scripture and are indeed used extensively as such, for the first time, by St Irenaeus.

CONTINUING TO SEARCH

In the chaos of the second century regarding the identity of Christ and the framework in which he is known, St Irenaeus articulated some basic principles which are equally applicable now. Indeed, one could say that a great deal of our modern confusion results from detaching the New

Testament from the constellation of elements—scripture (the Old Testament), canon, tradition, and succession—in which it came to be. Yet this framework is no more than just that—a framework within which one can come to know Christ and to respond in a meaningful way to the question that he poses: "Who do you say that I am?" (Mt 16.15).

The answer to this question does not lie in a historical analysis of the texts of the New Testament—to find out what they *meant*—but in responding to Christ now, discovering what scripture *means*. Christ remains the "coming one," who opens the scriptures to his disciples so that they can come to know him as Lord. This demands, of those who would be his disciples, a continuing engagement with the scriptures, in the context of tradition and following the rule of truth, an engagement in which the student of the Word is also "interpreted" by the Word as he or she puts on the identity of Christ. Tradition is the continuity of this interpretative engagement with the scriptures in the contemplation of Christ, as delivered ("traditioned") by the apostles . The faith delivered by the apostles "once for all" (Jude 3) is thus an active, dynamic movement. Tradition, therefore, is not a refuge, something that we can passively lay claim to, but a challenge, forcing us to engage with the scriptures to contemplate Christ, who always remains the coming one, learning to put on his identity, so that when he appears we shall be like him (1 Jn 3.2). Moreover, this is a task that cannot be avoided: even when John the Baptist was imprisoned and sent his disciples to ask Jesus "are you the coming one or shall we look for another?" Jesus did not give a straightforward answer, but directed him to signs—the blind seeing, the lame walking—which can only be understood as "messianic" through the interpretation of them by scripture (Mt 11.2–5).

This is a task which lies before every one who would respond to Christ. As we have seen, the appeal to a canon of truth was not meant to curtail thought, but to ensure that it did not dissolve into endless regression or mythology. The canon functions to make genuine theological reflection possible. "The rule did not limit reason to make room for faith, but used faith to make room for reason. Without a credible first principle, reason was lost in an infinite regress."[29] As Christ is the treasure hidden in the scriptures, the scriptures will themselves yield abundant riches as disciples continue to contemplate the precious pearl that is Christ. As St Ephrem of Syria, in the fourth century, put it:

> If there were [only] one meaning for the words [of scripture], the first interpreter would find it, and all other listeners would have neither the toil of seeking nor the pleasure of finding. But every word of our Lord has its own image, and each image has its own members, and each member possesses its own species and form. Each person hears in accordance with his capacity, and it is interpreted in accordance with what has been given to him.[30]

This is a creative task, to be engaged in by each generation as it appropriates the apostolic deposit and proclaims it anew under the inspiration of the same Spirit, so preserving the youthfulness of the Church. As St Irenaeus put it, the preaching of the prophets and apostles, preserved in the Church and received from the Church, is constantly renewed by the Spirit of God, "as if it were a precious deposit in an excellent vessel, so causing the vessel itself containing it [i.e., the Church] to be rejuvenated also."[31] That is, by preserving the preaching of the Church, the apostolic deposit, which the Spirit of God continually makes flourish, the Church herself is rejuvenated.

This tradition, with its own proper hypothesis and canon or creed, calls for continual reflection. In the centuries that followed Christians did so reflect and used all the means at their disposal. We now have many monuments to this continual engagement with the gospel proclaimed in accordance with the scriptures—writings of the Fathers and saints, schools of iconography and hagiography, and so on—all of which have a certain authority to the extent that they point to the same vision of the King, the gospel image of Christ. The Word grows, as Acts puts it

(Acts 6:7), in that as more and more people believe on it and reflect on it, there are ever new, more detailed and comprehensive explanations elaborated in defense of one and the same faith, the faith in what has been delivered from the beginning, the gospel according to the scriptures, the same Word of God—Jesus Christ, the same yesterday, today, and for ever (Heb 13:8).

In the light of the canon of truth itself, other elements are also called "canons": classical liturgical anaphoras epitomize the whole of scripture; hymnography poetically expounds the mystery of Christ; those saints whose lives and teachings embody the truth are "canons" of faith and piety; and the decisions of the councils concerning the proper order for the Church and people of God in particular situations are also considered "canons." Christians stand as heirs to all this wealth of tradition, which provides a nourishing structure but also offers a challenge: how to appropriate all of this wealth in such a way that it aids contemplation of the coming Christ, that is, keeps Christians oriented towards the future, for "our commonwealth is [still] in heaven, and from it we await our Savior, the Lord Jesus Christ, who will change [i.e., in the future] our lowly body to be like his glorious body" (Phil 3.20–1), rather than stuck in the past, as if the past had any value in itself, other than directing us (when seen with discernment) to Christ, the one to whom the Spirit and the Bride still say, "Come!" (Rev 22.17).

NOTES

[1]Tertullian *Against Marcion* 3.5.4. Ed. and trans. E. Evans, OECT (Oxford: Clarendon Press, 1972).

[2]Tertullian *The Prescription against the Heretics* 16. Ed. R. F. Refoulé and French trans. P. de Labriolle, SC 46 (Paris: Cerf, 1957); Eng. trans in ANF 3.

[3]St Cyprian of Carthage *Epistle* 74.9.2. Ed. and French trans. Canon Bayard (Paris: Les Belles Lettres, 1962); Eng. trans. in ANF 5 (where it is numbered ep. 73).

[4]R. Pfeieffer points to David Ruhnkin in 1768 as being the first to use the term "canon" in this way. See his *A History of Classical Scholarship* (Oxford: Clarendon Press, 1968), 207.

[5]Cf. H. Y. Gamble, *Books and Readers in the Early Church: A History of Early Christian Texts* (New Haven and London: Yale University Press, 1995), 58–65; T. C. Skeat, "The Oldest Manuscript of the Four Gospels?" *New Testament Studies* 43 (1997): 1–37; G. N. Stanton, "The Fourfold Gospel," *New Testament Studies* (1997): 317–46.

[6]See B. M. Metzger, *The Canon of the New Testament: Its Origin, Development, and Significance*, repr. with corrections (Oxford: Clarendon Press, 1989), Appendix 4 (pp. 305–15), for the scant evidence of such concern in antiquity.

[7]St Irenaeus of Lyons *Against the Heresies* 4.26.1. Ed. and French trans. A. Rousseau et al., SC 263–64, 293–94, 210–11, 100, 152–53 (Books 1–5 respectively) (Paris: Cerf, 1979, 1982, 1974, 1965, 1969). Eng. trans. in ANF 1.

[8]St Irenaeus *Against the Heresies* 1.8.1.

[9]Aristotle *Metaphysics* 5.1.2 (1013a17). Ed. and trans. H. Tredennick, LCL Aristotle 17–18 (Cambridge, MA: Harvard University Press, 1933).

[10]Aristotle *Metaphysics* 4.4.2 (1006a6–12).

[11]Clement of Alexandria *Stromata* 8.3 (8.3.6.7–7.2). *Stromata VII-VIII*. Ed. O. Stählin, 2nd ed. rev. L. Früchtel and U. Treu, GCS 17 (Berlin: Akademie Verlag, 1970). Trans. in ANF 2.

[12]Cf. *Stromata* 7.16 (7.16.95.4–6).

[13]St Irenaeus *Against the Heresies* 1.9.4.

[14]Aristotle *On the Soul* 1.5 (411a5–7). Ed. and trans. W. S. Hett, LCL Aristotle 8 (Cambridge, MA.: Harvard University Press, 1936).

[15]St Irenaeus *Against the Heresies* 1.10.1.

[16]Cf. *Against the Heresies* 1.8.1, cited earlier, and his *Demonstration of the Apostolic Preaching* 1, trans. J. Behr (Crestwood, NY: St Vladimir's Seminary Press, 1997).

[17]Clement of Alexandria *Stromata* 6.15 (6.15.125.3). *Stromata I–VI*. Ed. O. Stählin, 3rd ed. rev. L. Früchtel, GCS 52 (Berlin: Akademie Verlag, 1972). Trans. in ANF 2.

[18]St Irenaeus *Against the Heresies* 3.11.8.

[19]For the exegetical practices of the *Gospel of Truth*, see D. Dawson, *Allegorical Readers and Cultural Revision in Ancient Alexandria* (Berkeley: University of California Press, 1992).

[20]Cf. A. Louth, *Discerning the Mystery: An Essay on the Nature of Theology* (Oxford: Clarendon Press, 1983).

[21]St Irenaeus *Against the Heresies* 1.10.2.

[22]W. W. Harvey, in his edition of *Against the Heresies*, printed twelve years after J. H. Newman's *Essay on the Development of Christian Doctrine*, pointed out, in a footnote to this passage (1.10.2): "At least here there is no reserve made in favour of any theory of development. If ever we find any trace of this dangerous delusion in Christian antiquity, it is uniformly the plea of heresy." (Cambridge, 1857), 1. 94.

[23]St Irenaeus *Against the Heresies* 3.1.1–2.

[24]*Against the Heresies* 3.2.1.

[25]*Against the Heresies* 3.2.2, 3.4.

[26]*Against the Heresies* 3.3.3.

[27]Cf. *Against the Heresies* 3.12.9.

[28]*Against the Heresies* 3.5.1.

[29]E. Osborn, "Reason and the Rule of Faith in the Second Century AD," in R. Williams ed., *The Making of Orthodoxy: Essays in Honour of Henry Chadwick* (Cambridge: Cambridge University Press, 1989), 40–61, at p. 57.

[30]St Ephrem of Syria *Commentary on the Diatessaron* 7.22. Trans. C. McCarthy (Oxford: Oxford University Press, 1993).

[31]St Irenaeus *Against the Heresies* 3.24.1.

CHAPTER THREE

For This Were We Created

When the disciples encountered the risen Lord and began to understand the truth of God that he reveals, and indeed is, they were also confronted with the reverse side of this revelation: the truth that they had abandoned him at the time of his Passion. This is made most clear in the account provided by the Gospel of John. Here, after the Passion, the disciples are back at the lake fishing, as if nothing had happened. Jesus appears, at the break of day, but is only recognized when he directs them to the place that they can find sustenance, and find it in abundance; only then does the beloved disciple say to Peter: "It is the Lord" (Jn 21.4–7). But before Peter could again address Jesus as "Lord," he is confronted by Christ asking him three times, "Simon, son of John, do you love me?" (Jn 21.12, 15–17). Peter has to acknowledge his past, in which he denied Christ three times, as part of who he is; he cannot simply return to the more comfortable period before his time as a disciple, and a failed disciple at that. Only in this way can he once again be "Peter," the "rock" (the meaning of the name "Peter" in Greek) and his past failure be brought to a good conclusion in his work as an apostle.

These two episodes are linked in the Gospel of John by its description of their settings: Peter denies Christ while warming himself besides "a charcoal fire" (Jn 18.18, *anthrakia*); likewise, when he professes his love for Christ it is again by "a charcoal fire" (Jn 21.9), one which, together with the meal, was provided for them.[1] This is surely not accidental, for the Gospel of John is otherwise very sparse in such details, but is meant to recall the experience of Isaiah (who saw the glory of Christ and spoke of him, cf. Jn 12.41): after his vision of the enthroned Lord in the heavenly temple, Isaiah cried out, "Woe is me! For I am lost; for I am a man of unclean lips and I dwell in the midst of a people of unclean lips; for my eyes have seen the King, the Lord of Hosts," but then saw a seraphim place in his mouth a burning coal (*anthraka*) taken from the altar, with the words, "Behold this has touched your lips, your guilt is taken away and your sins forgiven" (Is 6.1–7). This encounter with the Lord and the subsequent recognition that one is a sinner, but a forgiven sinner, is the basic movement for further theological reflection.

This same movement is evident in the scriptural reports of the preaching of the Resurrection. The Resurrection is always proclaimed to a specific audience; it is not simply a matter of giving information, nor is it proclaimed to a neutral or innocent audience—there are no "uninvolved bystanders" in this. As it is presented in the book of Acts, the apostle Peter begins by addressing the "men of Judaea and all who dwell in Jerusalem," proclaiming that "this Jesus, delivered up according to the definite plan and foreknowledge of God, you crucified and killed by the hand of lawless men" (Acts 2.14, 23). Although it is according to the plan and knowledge of God (the movement to theology that we explored in Chapter One: he was not simply put to death, but gave himself up), nevertheless, it was "all those who dwell in Jerusalem" who actually crucified Jesus. It is to these that the apostles, who have now assimilated their own past, proclaim that the crucified Jesus is the exalted Lord, raised from the dead and sitting at (and as) the right hand of God, to which the only response is to repent, be baptized in the name of Jesus for the forgiveness of sins, and receive the gift of the Holy Spirit (Acts 2.24–38).

As the apostles continue to proclaim this message, they themselves are arrested and delivered on the following morning to "the rulers and elders and scribes gathered together in Jerusalem, with Annas the high priest and Caiaphas . . ." (Acts 4.5–6): they stand, in the name of Jesus, in the very court that condemned Jesus, proclaiming to the same court God's vindication of the one they condemned. In the words of the apostles, Jesus is returned to his judges as their judge. As long as this court, and the whole city, continue to reject their words, continue to judge and condemn, they bring upon themselves the judgment of their victim.

But this is not simply a reversal of roles, with the victim now becoming the judge. Rather, while being a lawless act of violence, this same act is also one that, seen theologically, is encompassed in "the plan and knowledge of God," and so the return of the exalted Lord, who is not merely a victim but the one who gave himself up for the life of the world, is a return which is not presented by the apostles as a threat, but as an invitation for forgiveness and the "times of refreshing" in the presence of the Lord (Acts 3.19). This divine grace is manifest when his betrayers, judges, and those who crucified him, turn to him (repent) to know him as their Savior. He is this because, as Peter affirms, following Isaiah, "when he suffered, he did not threaten" (1 Pet 2.23): in and through the sufferings we inflict, he does not condemn, resist, or exclude; he suffers violence, but never inflicts it—he is the lamb of God who bears the sin of the world (Jn 1.29). Such suffering is not merely passive—something forced upon Christ—but is voluntarily undertaken and, as such, is creative, making all things new (Rev 21.5).

As the preaching of the Resurrection extends beyond Jerusalem to those abroad, it spreads as a persecuted faith. Persecuting the Church, Saul is told that he is persecuting Jesus himself (Acts 9.5), and is then converted, regaining his sight, receiving the Holy Spirit, and being baptized, through one of the persecuted members of Christ (Acts 9.17). Those who receive the preaching of the apostles, and turn to Christ as their Savior, must also recognize in him *their* victim and themselves as needing the reconciliation that he alone offers. This brings a new depth of meaning to the biblical imagery of God making his own cause the plight of the oppressed and outcast: it is not simply the anonymous poor and weak who are victimized by rich and powerful others or unjust impersonal systems—and whose cause we might take up on behalf of God—but one who has suffered at *our* hands.

The unique, "once for all," nature of the work of God in the crucified and exalted Christ, his creative suffering, means that it is to him that all must turn and continually return: "We are, insistently and relentlessly, in Jerusalem, confronted therefore with a victim who is *our* victim."[2] What is embodied and enacted in Christ, though occurring at a specific historical moment and in a particular context, is nevertheless God's own work and, as such, eternal or timeless. The preaching of his crucifixion and resurrection is not restricted to the first century, any more than the raised Christ is merely a resuscitated human individual limited to historical and geographic boundaries. Rather, now that Christ is with God, and all authority in heaven and earth has been given to him, there is no place or time where he cannot be or cannot work: he is present, even now, to those who turn to him, as the victim of their own sins, and, as such, the one who is able to forgive and bring them into the life of God.

As with the disciples after the Resurrection, the primary locus for this encounter is a meal. The eucharistic celebration is not simply a fellowship meal or a commemoration of a past meal, but one which begins "in the same night in which he was given up": "We do not eucharistically remember a distant meal in Jerusalem, nor even a distant death: we are made 'present to ourselves' as people complicit in the betrayal and death of Jesus and yet still called and accepted, still companions of Christ in the strict sense—those who break bread with Him."[3] Through this recognition we enter into the companionship of the risen Christ—and he offers us a taste of a life not bound to death and hell. Only if we each approach the eucharistic cup as Isaiah received the burning coal, with the confession that I am indeed a sinner and, as the prayer before communion—following the apostle Paul (1 Tim 1.15)—puts it, "the chief of sinners," will we hear the words spoken to Isaiah and now said by the priest after we receive communion, "Behold this has touched your lips, your guilt is taken away and your sins forgiven" (Is 6.7). Only in this way will the eucharistic gifts be for us, as St Ignatius of Antioch describes them, "the medicine of incorruptibility."[4]

CREATION AND SALVATION

That Christ was "delivered up according to the definite plan and foreknowledge of God" (Acts 2.23), so that all could enter into the peace of God in the manner described above, invited later theologians to reflect further on the timeless work of God in Christ, seeing it as the very reason for creation. St Irenaeus of Lyons, at the end of the second century, put it in very striking terms:

> Since he who saves already existed, it was necessary that he who would be saved should come into existence, that the One who saves should not exist in vain.[5]

Such a statement today strikes us as odd. We tend to think in linear, historical terms, beginning with God having brought creation into being, followed by the first human beings, Adam and Eve, using their God-given freedom against their creator and so plunging the world into sin and mortality, a condition in which it languished while the work of salvation was gradually being prepared, culminating in the Incarnation of Christ. If, in this perspective, we affirm the unity of creation and salvation, it would be in the sense of the whole of creation being saved, or as the distinct events of creation and salvation both being fitted together into one salvation history under the control of the one God.

In the framework provided by such an approach, there has been much debate, especially in the renewed dialogue between Eastern and Western Christianity in the past century, regarding the content of the Fall and original sin. This debate has often turned upon the translation of Rom 5.12: "As sin came into the world through one man and death through sin, so death spread to all men, *eph o* all men sinned." If the Greek phrase *eph o* is taken as "in whom," as it was read by some Latin writers, then all human beings have sinned "in Adam" through their seminal identity with him, and his guilt, in turn, is passed down through all generations. If it is translated as "because" (as in the RSV), then it might be taken to imply that Adam's sin has resulted in the spread of mortality, through the fear of which we "were subject to lifelong bondage" (cf. Heb 2.15), a condition which impels each human being to sin. The value of this, it is claimed, has been to argue that though the "cosmic disease" of mortality infects the whole human race, nevertheless, sin remains a personal act, for which each is responsible.[6]

We have become so accustomed to speaking about "the Fall" that we have perhaps forgotten what it is that we are speaking about, or more exactly, *how* it is that we are speaking. In such discussions we tend to treat "the Fall" as if it were a historical event, one which could be correlated, for instance, to the Battle of Troy, and for which an account, some version of a theory of "original sin," needs to be given. We have, moreover, become used to asking counterfactual, hypothetical questions, such as the one which has surfaced with monotonous regularity since Thomas Aquinas and Duns Scotus, whether Christ would have become incarnate had there been no Fall. As we tend to speak of it, the Fall has resulted in an accidental alteration in the life of creation, resulting solely from free human will, such that St Irenaeus' statement, that we were brought into being in order to be saved, strikes us as confused and confusing, not to mention the fact that he does not even use the vocabulary of "Fall," preferring instead to use "apostasy" in striking terms that we will explore later.

Other Fathers also speak in similarly unsettling ways. St Athanasius, for instance, describes how, after they were created by God in his own image "through his own Word, our Savior Jesus Christ," human beings turned away from contemplating the Word, and he then brings in Adam, "the first of human beings," *as an example* of this.[7] St Maximus the Confessor affirms that the first man, "together with his coming-into-being," misused his God-given capacity for spiritual enjoyment so that his "first movement" was towards the things of sense-perception rather than his Creator, but that this was encompassed in God's overall providence for his creation: there never was a "time," for St Maximus, in which human beings did not stand in need of Christ.[8] In speaking in such ways, did the Fathers simply overlook, or not fully appreciate, what for us seems to be a given, "the Fall," an "event" subsequent to creation itself and the time in paradise, and for which an account needs to be given? Or is there something more, and something radically different, going on here?

We should consider again *how* it is that we speak about "the Fall." It might sound counterintuitive, but the starting point for the notion of "the Fall" is not the story of Adam and Eve in Genesis.[9] Although the Old Testament is well aware of the reality of sin and evil in the world, it does not explain this by referring to Adam and Eve. The writers of the Old Testament were quite capable of referring back to an earlier time for an explanation, as, for instance, when Isaiah says "your first father sinned" (43.27), though here the reference is probably to Jacob. In fact, the deed of Adam and Eve is not described, in Genesis, as "sin" (the term is first used in Gen 4.7, in the Lord's words to Cain), nor with similar words, such as "transgression" or "rebellion." The only period which has something in common with the customary picture of the Fall is the period before the Flood, when "The Lord saw that the wickedness of man was great in the earth, and that every imagination of the thoughts of his heart was only evil . . . the earth was corrupt in God's sight, and the earth was filled with violence" (Gen 6.5, 11). This is the only such statement in the Old Testament, but it is a world which was washed away: from this corrupt world God saved Noah and his kin, who, passing through the world in the ark, enter into a virtually new world (an image which, not surprisingly was taken as a type of baptism, cf. 1 Pet 3.20–21), the world in which we now live.

Moreover, the Old Testament assumes that it is possible not to sin. This is especially clear in the Psalms, where frequently the speaker declares himself to be free from all sin and evil, that he is not one of the many sinners and evildoers. For instance:

> I have kept the ways of the Lord and have not wickedly departed from my God. For all his ordinances were before me, and his statutes

> I did not put away from me. I was blameless before him, and I kept myself from guilt. Therefore the Lord has recompensed me according to my righteousness. (Ps 18.21–24)

The verses cited by Paul to establish that "all men, both Jews and Greeks, are under the power of sin" (Rom 3.9ff), all have a greatly restricted scope in their original setting, and indeed, Paul himself, referring to his situation before his conversion, says that he was "blameless with respect to righteousness under the law" (Phil. 3.6).

The same is true in regards to the issue of death. God certainly directed Adam not to eat of the tree of the knowledge of good and evil, warning that "in the day that you eat of it, you shall die" (Gen 2.17), while the serpent argued with Eve, claiming that "you will not die. For God knows that when you eat of it your eyes will be opened, and you will be like God, knowing good and evil" (Gen 3.4–5). They, of course, ate the fruit, so that their eyes were opened. But they did *not* die, certainly not on that day. Death is mentioned in the punishment of Adam (but not Eve or the serpent), when he is reminded that "you are dust, and unto dust you will return" (Gen 3.19). But the brunt of the punishment lies in his work; not in the work itself, for he was brought into the Garden to till the ground (cf. Gen 2.15), but in this work becoming burdensome, for the ground is now cursed because of him, a source of continuing frustration, bringing sweat to his brow (cf. Gen 3.17–19). Death itself, returning to the dust, is not the punishment; rather, it is the endless toil and its futility in which Adam now lives, with the earth producing thorns and thistles for him. Death is more the final expression of this futility, returning to the ground from which he is taken. Similarly in the case of Eve, death is not even alluded to, but that which she would have undergone anyway is now made painful (Gen 3.16).

"In that day" they did not die. The text of Genesis gives no suggestion that Adam and Eve were, prior to this moment, immortal and that "in that day" Adam "died" by becoming mortal. The warning of God is already a warning for mortals: do this, and you will die! When such a warning is given elsewhere in the Old Testament (as in 1 Kings 2.36–46), the execution happens immediately once the deed is known. Nor is it really accurate to interpret Adam's punishment in terms of a rupture in relations between God and human beings, a kind of "spiritual death," for God continues to talk with him and his descendants. Adam and Eve are not presented in Genesis as being immortal beings who by sin fell into mortality, but as mortal beings who had the chance of attaining immortality, yet by that very act failed.

Their privileged position, closer to the source of life than their descendents, is recognized by their longevity, although this is something shared by other figures before the Flood: it is after the Flood, not the expulsion from Eden, that the human life span decreases dramatically. Adam himself lived to be 930 old (Gen 5.5), seventy years short of a thousand, and others for equally long periods, with Methuselah being the longest lived, reaching 969 (cf. Gen 5.6–27); after the flood, however, life span decreased rapidly, with Abraham reaching one hundred and seventy-five years (Gen 25.8) and Moses only one hundred and twenty (Deut 34.7), and soon after seventy years was reckoned to be a full span of life.

Mortality, in fact, seems to be regarded as natural in the Old Testament. There are a couple of exceptions to the normal mortality of humans—Enoch (Gen 5.24) and Elijah (2 Kgs 2)—but they are the exceptions which prove the rule. In the Old Testament, death is not ubiquitously seen as a curse or a punishment for sin. In fact, the death of figures such as Abraham, whose lives are of significance for the unfolding of the narrative, are described in blessed terms: he "breathed his last and died in good old age, an old man and full of years, and was gathered to his people" (Gen 25.8). Such a death, surrounded by children and their children, and completed with a proper burial, is seen as natural and right, a completion and fulfillment, and, indeed, even grants the perpetuity of the deceased's name: "The days of a good life are numbered, but a good name endures forever" (Sir 41.13).

If it cannot be said that, in the Old Testament, death is always a curse for human beings, neither can it be said that death is the last enemy of God. Certainly the existence of death is not attributed to God in the creation accounts of Genesis, a point affirmed directly in the later Wisdom literature: "God did not create death, nor does he delight in the destruction of the living; for he created all things for being" (Wis 1.13–14). But neither did God create the darkness lying over the face of the deep, needing to be separated from the light (Gen 1.2–4). While God might not have created death, he is certainly prepared to use it. God is "the source of life" (Ps 36.9) and is occasionally described as "the living God" (though only twice in the Psalms, 42.2, 84.2), but he is also prepared to use death: "I kill and I make alive" (Deut 32.39). The psalm used to open every vespers service, which describes the majesty of God's creation (and which may well have been written before the opening chapter of Genesis), inscribes death into the very pattern and rhythm of creation:

> When you take away their breath, they die and return to their dust;
> when you send forth your Spirit, they are created. (Ps 104.29–30)

God is the giver of life, but there seems to be no expectation that this should be a life without limits.

A couple of important qualifications regarding death in the Old Testament need to be made. First, it was not human mortality that was repugnant to the sight of God before the Flood, needing to be washed away, but human wickedness, specifically that "the earth was filled with violence" (Gen 6.11). Likewise, it is not death itself from which the Psalmist requests to be spared, but death at the hands of violent men (cf. Ps 86.14, 140.1, 4). Violent death does not occur at the will of God and, as such, is unnatural and ungodly. The ungodliness of the violent man, and of violence itself, is a theme which runs throughout the Old Testament, and into the New Testament in important ways, as we will see.

Second, the Old Testament does use the term "death" in another, metaphorical or poetic, sense besides that of actual human death. If God stands opposed to the violence of men, what challenges him in return is "death" as an opposing force, seeking to ensnare human beings. For instance:

> The cords of death encompassed me, the torrents of perdition
> assailed me;
> the cords of Sheol entangled me, the snares of death confronted
> me. (Ps 18.4–5)

Such language possibly derives from older Ugaritic mythologies describing cosmic battles between God and "death" (the ancient Near-Eastern god Mot).[10] Yet in such passages (which are rare compared to the normal use of the word), the term "death" clearly does not refer to the end of a person's life, but to a metaphysical force opposing God, one which attempts to seize human beings, through sin, sickness, hostility, violence, exhaustion, and so on. The overcoming of this poetic "death" and the violence of the ungodly come together in the prophetic passages describing the hope of, and promise for, peace in the rule of God, perhaps on occasion (though seldom) hinting that even death in its normal sense might be vanquished: "He will swallow up death for ever" (Is 25.8; cf. Hos 13.14).

All that said, however, if the customary Christian understanding of "the Fall" (or at least some version of it) is not there in Genesis, or the Old Testament more generally, it certainly is there in the New Testament, in particular in the letters of the apostle Paul. But it is important here to acknowledge that what the apostle says about Adam's sin is based on his prior conviction that Christ is the savior of all. When Paul was persecuting the Church, he did not think that he stood in need of the Savior that they proclaimed: "as to zeal, a persecutor of the Church, as to righteousness under the law, blameless" (Phil 3.6). At this point, Paul was not waiting for a savior to deliver him from bondage to sin and death; at most the disciples were hoping for a political messiah, one who would restore the kingdom to Israel (cf. Lk 24.21; Acts 1.6). But then Christ confronted his persecutor in such a manner that, when his eyes were opened, he realized that God had acted in Christ to save the whole world, and so the only conclusion he could draw was that the world stood in need of salvation![11]

Put another way, the solution comes first, and then we begin to understand where the problem lies. Christ is, as we saw in the last chapter, the first principle or hypothesis for all Christian theology. In the light of God's action in Christ, the apostle Paul draws the typological parallel: "As sin came into the world through one man and death through sin, so death spread to all men because all men sinned" (Rom 5.12). While different theories have been advanced as to how death and sin spread to all human beings, each with their own strengths and weaknesses, it must never be forgotten that the basis for this claim is Christ's work of salvation.

As we have seen, theology moves from the historical statement, that Jesus Christ was put to death, to the theological affirmation that he gave himself up for the life of the world, so that the apostles can proclaim, in their message of salvation, that this Jesus whom "you crucified and killed by the hand of lawless men" was nevertheless "delivered up according to the definite plan and foreknowledge of God" (Acts 2.23). The apostle Paul takes this theological reflection, in the light of Christ, further, to affirm that even human apostasy, when viewed theologically, is in the hands of God. Realizing that if salvation has come through Christ, and righteousness through faith in Christ and not by the law (as is demonstrated by scripture in the person of Abraham), then the law must have had a different purpose, the apostle concludes, "Scripture consigned all things to sin, that what was promised to faith in Jesus Christ might be given to those who believe" (Gal 3.22): the disciples of Christ had the scriptures and so should have known the one of whom they speak; that they did not convicts them, but also prepares them to receive the mercy of Christ. As such, "sin" itself is now no longer defined in terms of the law, but in terms of being "in Adam" rather than "in Christ," and the whole human race "in Adam," without Christ, can be described in St Augustine's phrase as one "mass of sin," without implying a pessimistic view of humanity: it is the precondition of needing Christ, who comes "to call not the righteous, but the sinners" (Mt 9.13). Not only the giving of the law, but also all the other intervening events and figures described in scripture, can now be seen as part of a "salvation history" leading to Christ, already speaking of him and under his guidance.

When the apostle Paul says, in another place, that "God has consigned all men to disobedience, that he may have mercy on all," he concludes by marveling in wonder: "O the depth of the riches and wisdom and knowledge of God!" (Rom 11.32–3). Such statements are rarely taken into account in theories of the "Fall" and "original sin," and indeed it would be difficult to do so; there one would be more likely to speak of God consigning all to death once human beings turn away from him. But to do this, would be to envision creation without Christ, a creation in which, had human beings not sinned, there would have been no need for Christ. It would, in short, posit a hypothesis or first principle other than Christ himself, who, as the crucified and exalted Lord, opens the scriptures so that we can see the whole of creation and its history in his light. On this basis, the apostle Paul can view the sinfulness of human beings—and even the very creation of Adam, "a type of the one to come" (Rom 5.14), and the light which shone in darkness (Gen 1.3; 2 Cor 4.6)—within the overall plan of God which culminates in the Passion of his Son. Human weakness, and even death itself, are invested with profound new meaning by being elevated to a properly theological vision. There are no better words to express this than the doxology, the words of praise, opening the Letter to the Ephesians:

> Blessed be the God and Father of our Lord Jesus Christ, who has blessed us in Christ with every spiritual blessing in the heavenly places, even as he chose us in him before the foundation of the world, that we should be holy and blameless before him. He

> destined us in love to be his sons through Jesus Christ, according to the purpose of his will, to the praise of his glorious grace which he freely bestowed on us in the Beloved. In him we have redemption through his blood, the forgiveness of our trespasses, according to the riches of his grace which he lavished upon us. For he has made known to us in all wisdom and insight the mystery of his will, according to his purpose which he set forth in Christ as a plan for the fullness of time, to unite all things in him, things in heaven and things on earth. (Eph 1.3–10)

This is "the unsearchable riches of Christ" that the apostle proclaims, enabling all "to see what is the plan of the mystery hidden for ages in God who created all things," made known to the angels only through the Church, "the eternal purpose which he has realized in Christ Jesus our Lord" (Eph 3.8–11).

LOOKING BACKWARDS AT CREATION

With this perspective, we can now understand St Irenaeus' statement that "since he who saves already existed, it was necessary that he who would be saved should come into existence, that the one who saves should not exist in vain."[12] Viewed in the light of Christ, beginning with the Savior, creation and salvation are not two distinct actions, but the continual process of God's activity in his handiwork, bringing the creature, when he allows himself to be skillfully fashioned, to the stature of the Savior, by whom and for whom all creation has come into being. This process, as we will explore further, includes human apostasy, the acquisition of the knowledge of good and evil, the experience of sin and death.

Similarly, in presenting an apology for the Cross, demonstrating that "the one who ascended the cross is indeed the Word (*Logos*) of God" so that Christian faith is not irrational (*alogos*), St Athanasius extends this theological reflection to the very being of creation.[13] He affirms, on principle, that creation has been brought into being from nothing, *ex nihilo*, for nothing stands alongside the eternal and omnipotent God, independent of him; but the creation with which he is specifically concerned is that of the cosmos and the human race by the Word of God, "our Savior Jesus Christ."[14] Moreover, the reason for the Word having come to created being shows us, according to St Athanasius, "that things should not have occurred otherwise than as they are."[15] Athanasius takes this line of reflection to its limit when he asks, in very strong terms, what God was to do in the face of human apostasy:

> Be silent before such things, and let humans be deceived by demons and be ignorant of God? But then what need would there have been for the human being to have been created in the image from the beginning? . . . And what advantage would there be to God who made him, or what glory would he have, if humans who had been created by him did not honour him, but thought that others had made them?[16]

These are bold words indeed, suggesting that God has a "need" of creation, that it is to his "advantage," and that he would have no "glory" were it not for his creatures. But rather than imagining God prior to creation, to postulate some kind of primordial lack in God himself—as he exclaims, in a different context, "such is their mythology, for it is no theology, far from it!"[17]—St Athanasius begins with the given fact of the revelation of God in Christ, that which *is*, and, on this basis and in its terms, develops a theology and cosmology in which Jesus Christ is truly the beginning and end, and the glory which he receives and exhibits as the crucified one is the glory which he had with the Father from all eternity—for there is no other glory.

That speaking of "the Fall" begins with the encounter with Christ means that we should not too readily equate "salvation history" with "history" as we generally employ that term—a record of things as they "really happened," verifiable by other historical records, so constructing our own historical narrative, which we hold to be "true" by a criterion or canon of our own creation. As we have seen, it is *not* in terms of such a "salvation history" that Paul and the disciples of Christ read scripture prior to their encounter with the risen Lord, even if it certainly is thereafter. "Salvation history" is written from the perspective of the Cross, with its totality—creation, human sinfulness, the giving of the law, the preparation, and the work of salvation—simultaneously revealed in and through the proclamation of the crucified and risen Christ, the eternal plan or economy of God.

"Salvation history" certainly unfolds in scripture as a narrative, as we read from the opening verses of Genesis onwards, but reading this narrative as a "salvation history" is nonetheless a statement of how these scriptures appear retrospectively in the light of Christ. Ultimately, "salvation history" is based on, and truly is, a confession about Christ, the one who opens all the books of scripture to show how they speak of him and his Passion, and so, as we now confess, he is the one who has brought creation into being and guided its history, as spoken of in scripture, to its fulfillment in himself. The early iconographic depictions of creation, such as the marvelous mosaic in San Marco, Venice (Plate 2), give a vivid sense of how one can visualize creation coming into being and ordered by Christ, who is identified by the cross in his halo.

Approaching the mystery of Christ in this way, Paul can even speak, as we have seen, in terms of *our* election "before the foundation of the world" and of *our* having been "destined" to this. If such statements were made in any other way than retrospectively, on the basis of the encounter with Christ, it would make God into an arbitrary despot, who before creation decides who will be saved and who will not. But when one begins with the Savior Jesus Christ as the first principle, the hypothesis, what else can one conclude but that it is by him and for him that we have been brought into being?

Encompassing human sinfulness within this theological scope does not, however, remove our own personal responsibility: only when they were confronted with the one they had indeed denied and persecuted, did Peter and Paul know themselves as needing, and being offered, salvation. But the theological vision offered by the mystery of Christ elevates us to a height from which we can see our apostasy and sin as the arena in which God works, effecting a transformation that reveals the glory of God. As we saw in Chapter One, St Gregory of Nyssa affirmed that the power of God is made manifest in that which is external to him: in flesh, in darkness and in death, as Word, Light, and Life.[18] This transcendent, eternal or timeless, power of God enables us to see human sinfulness embraced within the whole scriptural economy of God, in a simultaneous movement of conviction and forgiveness, revealing our fallenness—that we have always stood in need of Christ, called into being by and for him—and yet in the same movement offering us the means by which our brokenness may be healed. In this retrospective perspective, we can speak of the "Fall" as being "blessed," the *felix culpa*,[19] and see the "curse" of Adam and Eve, as depicted in the San Marco mosaic (Plate 2), as a "blessing," with Christ making the sign of the cross over his repentant creatures.

So far we have only looked at the Creation and Fall as they appear in the scriptural narrative of "salvation history," contemplating the whole economy of God, as narrated in scripture, with the Passion of Christ as our first principle, our hypothesis. But the movement that we have been tracing opens out into a universal perspective on the whole of creation and its history. Just as any history is written retrospectively, with the benefit of hindsight and leading to the point from which it was written, so creation itself and the history of the world (or the multitude of histories asserted in today's world), when viewed from the encounter with Christ, are known as having been always guided by his providence in such a way that it finds its source and fulfillment in him. It does so in a manner that also includes the necessary moment of conviction—the consignment of all to sin and disobedience—to prepare for the reception of the gospel. Speaking of those who were not entrusted with the scriptures, Paul asserts: "What can be known about God is plain to them, because God has shown it to them. Ever since the creation of the world his invisible nature, namely, his eternal power and deity, has been clearly perceived in the things that have been made" (Rom 1.19–20). Although this is often taken as implying a possibility of "natural theology," that is, a knowledge of God apart from his revelation, from "nature" without a proper (theological) interpretation, the conclusion Paul draws is the opposite: "So they are without excuse"—they could have known God, but instead preferred the creature to the Creator (Rom 1.20ff). Again, only retrospectively can we see the power of God in the whole of creation in the form of the cross that, as St Justin Martyr points out, echoed by many others, is found everywhere, even in the banners of the Roman army and the structure of the human face.[20]

We can only speak of creation as having been brought into being by and for its savior Jesus Christ, and its whole history as having been providentially guided by him, from the moment that he is revealed within its history, at the Passion. Theologically speaking, creation and its history begins with the Passion of Christ and from this "once for all" work looks backwards and forwards to see everything in this light, making everything new. Christian cosmology, elaborated as it must be from the perspective of the Cross, sees the Cross as impregnated in the very structure of creation: *stat crux dum volvitur orbis*—the Cross stands, while the earth revolves. The power of God revealed in and through the Cross brought creation into being and sustains it in existence. As St Isaac of Syria commented,

> We do not speak of a power in the Cross that is any different from that through which the worlds came into being, [a power] which is eternal and without beginning and which guides creation all the time without any break, in a divine way and beyond the understanding of all, in accordance with the will of his divinity.[21]

Just as the date of the Passion of Christ in antiquity was considered to be 25 March (which, as we will see in the next chapter, was the basis for calculating the date of his nativity, nine months later), so also in antiquity 25 March was considered to be the very date of creation, the Creation which revolves around the axis of the eternal, immovable Cross.[22] As paradoxical as it might sound, one can say, theologically, that creation and salvation were effected simultaneously on that day, 25 March, AD 33, when Christ gave himself for the life of the world.

The change brought about by the Passion of Christ does indeed make all things new. The disciples no longer read the scriptures in the same way as before; now, in the light of the risen Christ, they read scripture differently, as the "salvation history" that we have been examining. Likewise, as we look more broadly at the whole of creation and its history, we see it in a new light, as having been brought into being by Christ and moving towards him as its fulfillment. Commenting on the change in the reading of scripture brought about by Christ, Origen makes a comment which can be taken more broadly:

> Before the sojourn of Christ, the law and the prophets did not contain the proclamation which belongs to the definition of the gospel, since he who explained the mysteries in them had not yet come. But since the Savior has come and has caused the gospel to be embodied, he has by the gospel made all things as gospel.[23]

He qualifies this statement later on, specifying that while the prophets (including Moses) did indeed know the grace which would be given in Christ, they veiled their message so as not to pre-empt the newness of the gospel.[24] While this would not persuade those who are not already persuaded of and by Christ, for those who have come to know Christ, the only conclusion that can be drawn is that he is indeed the one spoken of by the scriptures and the Lord of all creation and history. Seen, retrospectively, in his light, all is indeed filled with his light and speaks of his gospel.

It was through the encounter with the risen Christ, the one that they had betrayed and persecuted, that the apostles were able to understand the scope of salvation history, that they are fallen, but also offered forgiveness and resurrected life. If we are to follow in their steps, we should not begin with a claim to know ourselves as sinful and then find a savior who corresponds to what we think our problems are. Were we to do this, the end would assuredly be worse than the beginning. We may well sense that we have our own problems, and that all is not right with the world, yet *how* it is that we are sinful and fallen, and that the depth of our brokenness extends to the very core of our being, is not at all clear to us until we encounter Christ, the one who called, and calls, us into being and life. Christ provides the diagnosis of our condition and simultaneously provides the remedy. The proclamation of the crucified and risen Lord brings together all the brokenness of our life, unifying it, as it were, so that it can now be seen as a whole, recapitulated in a single vision, as our own salvation history in which he has led us to himself. Only in this way will we be able to open ourselves to the forgiveness and abundant life offered by the one who has taken our brokenness upon himself, in his broken body, nailing it to his cross—for it is by *his* Cross that this unity has been achieved and by *his* Cross that salvation is offered—and so allow our lives to be transformed, transfigured, resurrected. Salvation history, both that narrated in scripture and that of our own past, shaped now by the apostolic preaching of Christ according to the scriptures, is written upon and from the Cross, the exaltation of Christ.

"MY STRENGTH IS MADE PERFECT IN WEAKNESS"

"Law came in to increase the trespass; but where sin increased, grace abounded all the more, so that, as sin reigned in death, grace also might reign through righteousness to eternal life through Jesus Christ our Lord" (Rom 5.20–21). This principle does not grant, as the apostle Paul subsequently makes clear, a license to sin. It does, however, allow us to see the wisdom of God at work in our "consignment to sin" (Gal 3.22). The words of Christ to the apostle, that "my strength is made perfect in weakness" (2 Cor 12.9), provided a general principle by which the early Fathers were able to gain further insight into this aspect of the mystery of Christ.

Regarding the role of human apostasy—turning away from God to a life of sin—St Irenaeus points out that this now requires human beings to struggle, if they are to acquire a knowledge of God and to live in a manner befitting such knowledge. But this struggle is itself valuable, for endeavor heightens the appreciation of the gift. Moreover, as the faculty of seeing is desired more by those who know what it is like to be without sight, so also is health prized more by those who know disease, light by contrast with darkness, and life by death.[25] St Irenaeus develops this insight by contrasting two types of knowledge: that gained through experience and that arrived at by opinion. As the tongue learns of bitterness and sweetness only through experience, so also human beings acquire a knowledge of the good through the experience of both good and evil. Through experiencing both, and casting away disobedience through repentance, human beings become ever more tenacious in their obedience to God; but if they try to avoid the knowledge of both of these, they will forget themselves and kill their humanity.[26] Pointing out that the heavenly kingdom is more precious to those who have known the earthly kingdom, and, if they prize it more, so also will they love it more, and loving it the more, they will be more glorified by God, St Irenaeus concludes:

> God therefore has borne all these things for our sake, in order that, having been instructed through all things, henceforth we may be scrupulous in all things and, having been taught how to love God rationally [*logikōs*], remain in his love: God exhibiting patience in regard to the apostasy of human beings, and human beings being

> taught by it, as the prophet says: "Your own apostasy shall educate you" [Jer 2.19].

Irenaeus immediately continues by placing this particular action of God within the economy as a whole:

> God, thus, determining all things beforehand for the perfection of human beings, and towards the realization and manifestation of his economies, that goodness may be displayed and righteousness accomplished, and that the Church may be "conformed to the image of his Son" [Rom 8.29], and that, finally, the human being may be brought to such maturity as to see and comprehend God.[27]

So, for St Irenaeus, the aim of the whole economy, including the apostasy, is twofold: first, that human beings may be brought to perfection, to a maturity in which they can truly know God; and, second, this perfecting of the creature at the same time manifests the workings of God, displaying his goodness and justice.

St Irenaeus also includes death within this economy, as part of the knowledge of good and evil acquired by human beings in their growth towards maturity and in so doing provides a further insight into the educative role of the struggle in which human beings, from the beginning, find themselves. Approaching the subject from a different angle, as a rhetorical argument, he argues that God could have created human beings perfect or as "gods" from the beginning, for all things are possible to him. However, created things, by virtue of being created, are necessarily inferior to the One who created them, and so fall short of the perfect: they are of a later date, infantile (St Irenaeus depicts Adam and Eve as infants), and so unaccustomed to, and unexercised in, perfect conduct. Yet, as it is possible for a mother to give an infant solid food, so also God could have made human beings "perfect" from the beginning, but they, still in their infancy, could not have received this perfection.[28] Not that the omnipotence of God is restricted by the nature of that on which he is working, nor that the infantile state, despite only beginning to grow towards its full perfection, is itself imperfect. As a creature, human beings can never be uncreated, can never cease existing in the mode proper to a creature, that is, *being created.* But the aim of this creating or fashioning of human beings is that they should come to be ever more fully in the image and likeness of the uncreated God. There can be, for human beings, no end to this process; they can never become uncreated. Their perfection lies, instead, in their continual submission to the creative activity of God, through which they are brought to share in the glory of the Uncreated.[29] Finally, Irenaeus concludes by sketching the whole economy in a few brief strokes:

> It was necessary, first, for nature to be manifest; after which, for what was mortal to be conquered and swallowed up by immortality, and the corruptible by incorruptibility, and for the human being to be made in the image and likeness of God, having received the knowledge of good and evil.[30]

Creation and salvation, the appearance of human nature and the vanquishing of mortality by immortality, belong to the same economy, the purposeful arrangement, in which the acquisition of the knowledge of good and evil has its place, contributing to the realization, in the end, of the original divine intention of fashioning the creature made from mud into the image and likeness of God.

For further consideration of the role specifically of death within the economy of God, we need to attend to the distinction, discussed earlier in this chapter, between the two ways in which the word "death" can be used: the actual death of human beings, returning to the dust from which they were created, and the poetic or metaphorical "death" as a powerful force opposing God and holding us in its bondage. It is this form of death, rather than death itself, that is of crucial importance in understanding the value of Christ's death in the New Testament: Christ did not simply die, he died a death on the cross (Phil. 2.8). Similarly, the very structure of the Gospels—the length and details given to the passion narratives—indicate that what is of importance is not simply that Christ died, but the *way* in which he died, as an innocent victim, something which is intimately linked, as we have now seen, with Christ's role as Savior.

While these two senses of the word "death" are, with a couple of possible exceptions, held apart in the Old Testament, they are brought together explicitly in the apostolic proclamation that the crucified—the innocent victim of a violent death—has been raised bodily from the dead. Not only does Christ's manner of death, as the innocent victim, enable our liberation from enslavement to death, in its metaphorical sense–something looked upon as unnatural from the beginning—but his bodily death and resurrection now establishes the unnaturalness of our actual bodily death, and therefore the hope of our bodily resurrection. These two important aspects are intimately related, though we must treat them separately to investigate the fullness of this mystery.

Our liberation from death taken in a metaphorical sense is made clear in the New Testament, especially in the passages of the apostle Paul describing baptism. How can we continue in sin, he asks, now that we have died to sin?

> Do you not know that all of us who have been baptized into Christ Jesus were baptized into his death? We were buried therefore with him by baptism into death, so that as Christ was raised from the dead by the glory of the Father, we too might walk in newness of life. For if we have been united with him in a death like his, we shall certainly be united with him in a resurrection like his. We know that our old self was crucified with him so that the sinful body might be destroyed, and we might no longer be enslaved to sin. For he who has died is freed from sin. But if we have died with Christ, we believe that we shall also live with him. For we know that Christ being raised

COLOR PLATES

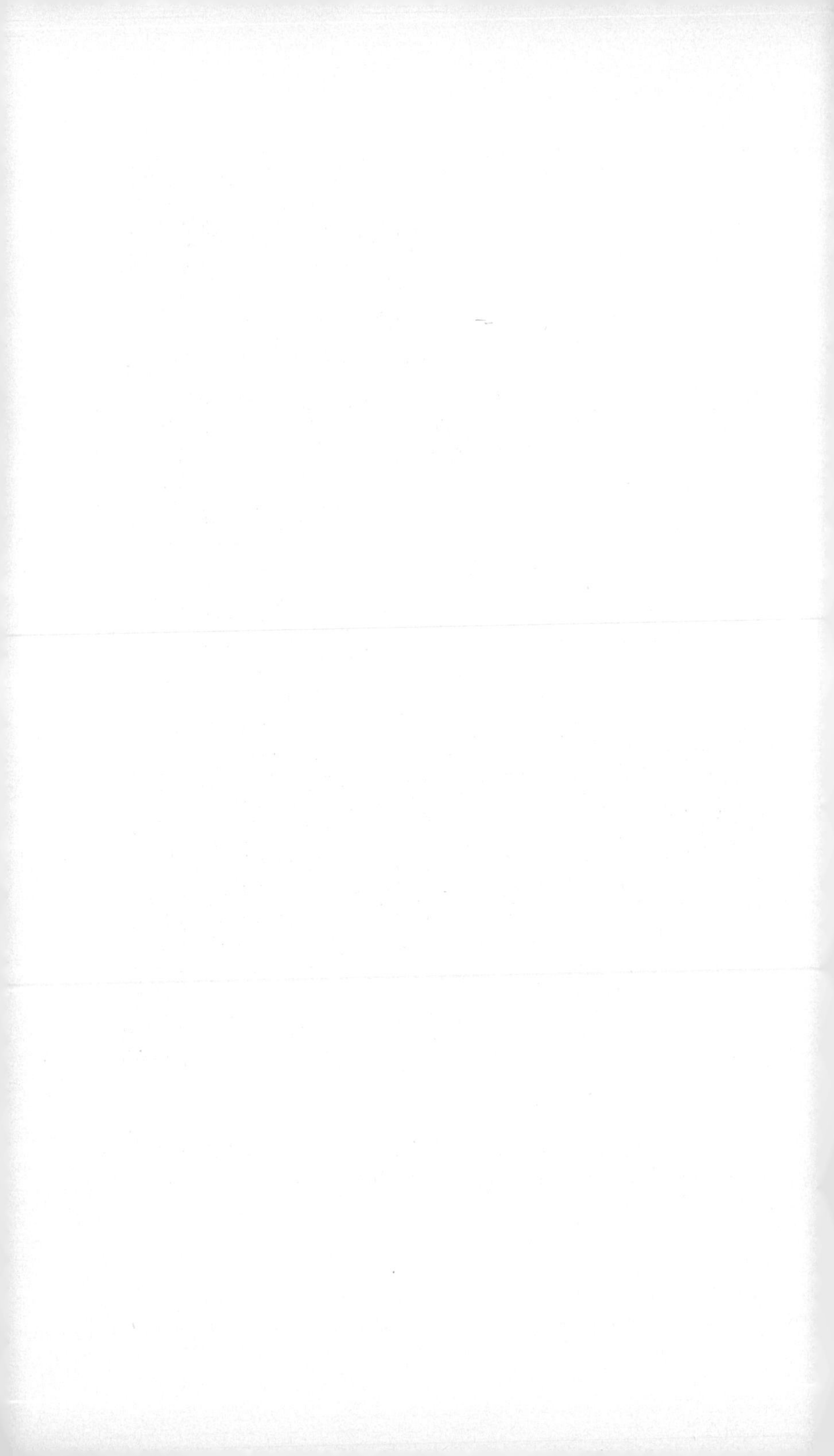

PLATE 1

Illustration of the Crucifixion of the Living Christ, from the Rabbula Gospels, AD 586, Cod. Plut. 1, 56, fol. 13r, Biblioteca Laurenziana, Florence. Scala/Art Resource.

PLATE 2

The Creation, thirteenth century mosaic, narthex cupola, San Marco, Venice. Scala/Art Resource.

PLATE 3

The Anastasis (Resurrection) of Christ, Russian, fourteenth century, Temple Gallery: London. St Vladimir's Seminary Press.

PLATE 4

The Virgin Orans and Christ Child, fresco in lunette, Catacomb of S.M. Maggiore, Rome. Scala/Art Resource.

PLATE 5

Icon with the Crucifixion and Nativity, late 13th–early 14th century. The Holy Monastery of Saint Catherine, Sinai, Egypt. Photograph by Bruce White. Photograph © 2003 The Metropolitan Museum of Art.

> from the dead will never die again; death no longer has dominion over him. The death he died he died to sin, once for all, but the life he lives he lives to God. So you also must consider yourselves dead to sin and alive to God in Christ Jesus. (Rom 6.3–11)

While Christ has already died, we are to *consider* ourselves as dead to sin and alive to God: "Do not yield your members to sin, as instruments of wickedness, but yield yourselves to God as men who have been brought from death to life, and your members to God as instruments of righteousness" (Rom 6.13). Yet we are still under death, and so, while our death to sin in baptism is spoken of as an event in the past, our life with Christ is still in the future: if we have died with Christ, through baptism, we shall also live with him.

The bondage in which we are held captive by death and the devil is described clearly in the Letter to the Hebrews, which also, more than any other New Testament text, emphasizes the suffering of Christ as the innocent victim. It is the purpose of Jesus, it says

> that through death he might destroy him who has the power of death, that is, the devil, and deliver all those who through fear of death were subject to lifelong bondage. . . . Therefore he had to be made like his brethren in all respects, so that he might become a merciful and faithful high priest in the service of God, to make expiation for the sins of the people. For because he himself has suffered and been tempted, he is able to help those who are tempted. (Heb 2.24–28)

We have been delivered from the bondage in which we were held captive, by the fear of death, through one who has suffered as we suffer, yet remained faithful, when we turn to him as our own victim. Through this recognition, we enter into the companionship of the risen Christ, and he offers us a taste of a life, a resurrected life, not bound to death and hell—"the medicine of incorruptibility," in St Ignatius' words.[31]

There is an intimate unity and intrinsic connection between the Resurrection of Christ and our own resurrection, both from our metaphorical death and also our eventual bodily death. The Resurrection of Christ was not depicted in early Christian art until the end of the seventh century. The triumph of Christ over death was represented instead by the depiction of the triumphant, living Lord on the cross, the empty tomb, and his appearances to the myrrh-bearing women (e.g., see Plate 1, discussed in Chapter One). Only later, perhaps in the ninth century, as images of the Resurrection became more prevalent, did the conservative iconographic tradition produce an image of the dead Christ on the cross. But the icon of the Resurrection of Christ, the *Anastasis* (Plate 3), does not actually depict Christ's bodily rising out of the tomb. It seems, instead, to portray Christ's descent into the underworld, a feature that has often led to it being misleadingly called "Descent into Hell" or the "Harrowing of Hell"; misleadingly, that is, because the scene depicted therein is consistently called, either on the icon itself or verbal descriptions, the *Anastasis*. The resurrection it speaks of is in fact that of Adam or the human race "in Adam" effected by Christ's Passion. While iconographers did not hesitate to depict other major events in the life of Christ—his Baptism, Transfiguration, Entry into Jerusalem—their treatment of the Resurrection, proceeds otherwise, portraying the effect of Christ's Passion, destroying of death by death, giving life to those in death. This is, moreover, something that has not yet been fully completed: Adam is in the process of being pulled out of the realm of death.[32]

The early Fathers similarly spoke in striking terms of the connection between the Resurrection of Christ and our resurrection from death, metaphorical death in the present and physical death in the end. St Ignatius, for instance, directs us to "give heed to the prophets and especially to the gospel, in which the Passion has been revealed to us and the resurrection has been accomplished":[33] the Resurrection is "accomplished" in the gospel proclamation, as we are now freed from bondage to death by dying, in Christ, to sin and its tyranny. In like manner,

St Athanasius, in his classic work *On the Incarnation*, after speaking at length about the Passion of Christ, does not even mention the resurrectional appearances of Christ as they are narrated in the Gospels (and on which we today tend to rely for confirmation that Christ did indeed rise from the dead). Rather he turns to present-day Christians, those who "take up the faith of the Cross" and "tread death underfoot, no longer fearing it, but with the sign of the cross and by faith in Christ trample on it as a dead thing," preparing, by ascetic exercises to bear witness to Christ even in their own death.[34] It is not the mark of a dead man, he continues, to persuade others to believe in him, to persuade them to live a righteous life and despise the idols they formerly worshipped: it is Christians themselves who are the witnesses of Christ's resurrection. This liberation from sin and the bondage of death is described by St John Climacus as "the resurrection of the soul prior to that of the body," manifest in those who have attained a dispassionate state, no longer swayed by the things of this world or the movements of our soul and body, something to which we will return in the final chapter.[35]

So far, we have spoken only spoken of "death" in the metaphorical sense, as the power of bondage from which we have been liberated by Christ's own Passion, a liberation which is also a manifestation of his victory over death. But this victory was not only over a "metaphorical" death, for he rose bodily from the dead to sit with the Father. This victory over both aspects of death enables us to see a further aspect to the mystery of Christ in our actual bodily death: the sowing of the mortal body in the ground so that, dying, it may rise as a spiritual body (1 Cor 15.35–57). There may well be a sense in which, even now, we might regard death as "natural," and count as blessed a death in good circumstances, as we saw it in the Old Testament considered by itself. It might be argued that this view would be a pastoral position to adopt when dealing with the bereaved. However, one finds a more categorical position in the words of St John of Damascus sung at the funeral service:

> I weep and I wail when I think upon death, and behold our beauty, fashioned after the image of God, lying in the tomb, disfigured, dishonored, bereft of form. O marvel! What is this mystery which befalls us? Why have we been given over unto corruption, and why have we been wedded to death? Of a truth, as it is written, by the command of God, who gives the departed rest.[36]

Death, and especially a good death, might, in one sense, be a natural end to life, but in a Christian perspective, it is always a catastrophe. Yet even here, in the midst of this catastrophe, as St John hints, there is a reason behind it: we are given over to death, by the command of God, and this is a marvel and a "mystery," the Greek word which in liturgical contexts is usually translated as "sacrament."

After baptism, being united with Christ "in the likeness of his death," Christians are called to bear witness to Christ's own resurrection by themselves dying to sin (a metaphorical death) in the confidence that they shall also be united with Christ in the resurrection in the age to come (cf. Rom 6.5). The Holy Spirit has been bestowed in Christ, and dwells in Christians now, preparing them for the resurrection: "If the Spirit of him who raised Jesus from the dead dwells in you, he who raised Christ Jesus from the dead will give life to your mortal bodies also through his Spirit which dwells in you" (Rom 8.11). The resurrectional life of Christ begins, this side of the grave, in the life of a continual dying to this world, this world, that is, as it stands opposed to God. While "the resurrection of the soul" may be attained in this world, becoming a true witness to Christ's own resurrection, the body itself must still die before it is raised again.

There are various aspects to this "mystery" of bodily death. The first is what we learn from the experience of death itself, in its educative role. Until we lie with our bodies decomposing in the grave—the dust that we are returning to the dust from which we were created—our temptation will always be to think that we have life in and from ourselves. Even if we practice "dying daily," dying to sin and that which stands opposed to God, we can only express this as *my* action of dying! But when we are finally dead in the ground, then it is, to paraphrase the apostle Paul, no longer I who works, but God who works in me—then God can finally be the creator.

It is precisely this educative role of death that St Irenaeus, beginning with the Passion of Christ and viewing "salvation history" in his light, explored with great insight. In a manner similar to his treatment of the apostasy, considered above, St Irenaeus asserts that God was patient with the human apostasy, as he foresaw the victory which would be granted to the human race through the Word: as strength is made perfect in weakness (2 Cor 12.9), God demonstrates his goodness and magnificent power in and through our own weakness and mortality. St Irenaeus gives as an example of this Jonah, who, by God's arrangement, was swallowed up by the whale, not that he should thus perish, but that, having been cast out, he might be more obedient to God, and so glorify more the God who had saved him. So also, Irenaeus continues:

> From the beginning, God did bear human beings to be swallowed up by the great whale, who was the author of transgression, not that they should perish altogether when so engulfed, but arranging in advance the finding of salvation, which was accomplished by the Word, through the "sign of Jonah" [Mt 12.39–40], for those who held the same opinion as Jonah regarding the Lord, and who confessed, and said, "I am a servant of the Lord, and I worship the Lord God of heaven, who made the sea and the dry land" [Jonah 1.9], that human beings, receiving an unhoped-for salvation from God, might rise from the dead, and glorify God, and repeat, "I cried to the Lord my God in my affliction, and he heard me from the belly of Hades" [Jonah 2.2], and that they might always continue glorifying God, and giving thanks without ceasing for that salvation which they have obtained from him, "that no flesh should glory in the Lord's

> presence" [1 Cor 1.29], and that human beings should never adopt an opposite opinion with regard to God, supposing that the incorruptibility which surrounds them is their own by nature, nor, by not holding the truth, should boast with empty superciliousness, as if they were by nature like to God.[37]

So, for St Irenaeus, God has borne the human race, from the beginning, while it was swallowed up by the whale. Although God did not actually create the human race *in* this condition, there was, nevertheless, no period of time before which human beings were not engulfed: there is, for St Irenaeus, no lost golden age of primordial perfection. This is not to deny that human beings themselves transgressed or apostatized, nor that there was an "author of transgression." The temptation for human beings is to think that the life they have is theirs by nature. Likewise, the devil's temptation is to offer what he could not give: Adam and Eve were beguiled under "the pretext of immortality."[38] Thus death is the result of human apostasy, turning away from the one and only Source of life; and at the same time it is the expression of the devil's dominion over the human race. But it is also embraced within the divine economy: when viewed from the perspective of the salvation granted by Christ through "the sign of Jonah," we can see that, as it was God himself who appointed the whale to swallow up Jonah, so also the engulfing of the human race by the great whale was "borne" by God in his arrangement, his economy, which culminates in the finding of salvation.

As the newly created humans were inexperienced, so they immediately gave way to temptation. But just as Jonah was swallowed by the whale that he might learn the true attitude to take with respect to God, so also, the human race was engulfed from the beginning as part of the divine economy, as an educational process, instructing us in the proper attitude towards God, culminating in an unhoped-for, but nonetheless divinely foreseen salvation, accomplished by the Word through the "sign of Jonah." This education, the whole of the divine economy, thus acquaints humans both with their own weakness, their total dependence on God, and also, and at the same time, with the strength and graciousness of God. As St Irenaeus continues:

> Such then was the patience of God, that human beings, passing through all things and acquiring knowledge of death, then attaining to the resurrection from the dead, and learning by experience from whence they have been delivered, may thus always give thanks to the Lord, having received from him the gift of incorruptibility, and may love him the more, for "he to whom more is forgiven, loves more" [cf. Lk 7.42–3], and may themselves know how mortal and weak they are, but also understand that God is so immortal and powerful as to bestow immortality on the mortal and eternity on the temporal, and that they may also know the other powers of God made manifest in themselves, and, being taught by them, may think of God in accordance with the greatness of God. For the glory of the human being is God, while the vessel of the workings of God, and of all his wisdom and power is the human being.[39]

God was thus patient while humans learned by experience their own weakness and death in their ungrateful apostasy, knowing that having passed through this experience, and having an unhoped-for salvation bestowed upon them, they would remain ever more thankful to God, willing to accept from him the eternal existence which he alone can give. In this way, human beings become fully acquainted with the power of God: reduced to nothing, to dust in the earth, human beings come to know their total dependency upon God, allowing God to work in and through them, to deploy his power in them as the recipient of all his work. Both dimensions of this economy—the engulfing of man, and the salvation wrought by the Word—are simultaneously represented by Jonah, a sign of both the transgressing human race and its Savior. In this way, human death has an educational role to play within the divine economy, enabling humans to experience to the uttermost their weakness and mortality in their apostasy from God, the only Source of life, so that they might thereafter hold ever more firmly to God.

Death plays a further role in this educational economy of God, as it is also the means of limiting the reign of sin. If death has come into the world as a result of sin (Rom 5.12), in reverse, death can also be seen as a restriction of sin: death cuts sin short, lest sin be immortal and as such unable to be healed. Viewed in this way, death can be seen not so much as an arbitrary penalty imposed for disobedience, nor as a consequence of human transgression—their turning away from the Source of life and so becoming mortal—but as a limitation on sin and death itself. As such, subjection to death can be seen as an act of mercy: it puts an end to sin through the resolution of man into the earth. Theophilus of Antioch, in the latter part of the second century, first arrives at this insight:

> It was not that the tree of knowledge contained anything evil, but that through disobedience man acquired pain, suffering and sorrow, and finally fell victim to death. And in so doing, God conferred a great benefit upon the human being. He did not let him remain for ever in a state of sin, so that through this punishment he might expiate his sin in a fixed period of time and after chastisement might later be recalled.[40]

This interpretation of the role of death within the divine economy is found in many Fathers thereafter. One further example of this is that of St Gregory of Nyssa:

> Suppose that some vessel has been composed of clay, and then, for some mischief or other, filled with molten lead, which lead hardens and remains in a non-liquid state; then that the owner of the vessel recovers it, and, as he possesses the potter's art, pounds to bits the ware which held the lead, and then remolds the vessel after its

> former pattern for his own special use, emptied now of the material which had been mixed with it: by a like process the maker of our vessel, now that wickedness has intermingled with our sentient part, I mean that connected with the body, will dissolve the material which has received the evil, and, remolding it again by the resurrection without any admixture of the contrary matter, will recombine the elements into the vessel in its original beauty.[41]

In this approach, then, death has a positive role to play, one might even say a remedial role: having learned by their own experience the utter weakness of their life in apostasy, without God, and so turning to God ever more firmly as the only Source of life, death terminates the apostasy, returning human beings to the dust from which they were taken, so that the traces of sin and apostasy can be purged from their body, and the human being can be refashioned in the resurrection.

There is one further aspect to the mystery of death, when seen in the light of the mystery of Christ, and that is to see it in eucharistic terms. The life in death, begun by dying to sin in baptism as a "likeness" of Christ's death (Rom 6.5), finds fruition in the eucharistic self-offering of the Christian in his or her own bodily death in witness to Christ. This finds striking expression in St Ignatius, when he beseeches the Christians in Rome not to interfere with his impending martyrdom:

> Suffer me to be eaten by the beasts, through whom I can attain to God. I am God's wheat, and I am ground by the teeth of wild beasts that I may be found pure bread of Christ.[42]

St Irenaeus develops this imagery much more fully:

> Just as the wood of the vine, planted in the earth, bore fruit in its own time, and the grain of wheat, falling into the earth and being decomposed, was raised up by the Spirit of God who sustains all, then, by

> wisdom, they come to the use of humans, and receiving the Word of God, become Eucharist, which is the Body and Blood of Christ; in the same way, our bodies, nourished by it, having been placed in the earth and decomposing in it, shall rise in their time, when the Word of God bestows on them the resurrection to the glory of God the Father, who secures immortality for the mortal and bountifully bestows incorruptibility on the corruptible [cf. 1 Cor 15.53], because the power of God is made perfect in weakness [cf. 2 Cor 12.9], that we may never become puffed up, as if we had life from ourselves, nor exalted against God, entertaining ungrateful thoughts, but learning by experience that it is from his excellence, and not from our own nature, that we have eternal continuance, that we should neither undervalue the true glory of God nor be ignorant of our true nature, but we should know what God can do and what benefits human beings, and that we should never mistake the true understanding of things as they are, that is, of God and of the human being.[43]

There is clearly a close relationship between the dynamism and fruitfulness of the Spirit and the action of the Word operative in the processes that lead both to the Eucharist and to the resurrection. It is by receiving the Eucharist, as the wheat and the vine receive the fecundity of the Spirit, that we are prepared, as we also make the fruits into the bread and wine, for the resurrection effected by the Word, at which point, just as the bread and wine receive the Word and so become the Body and Blood of Christ, the Eucharist, so also our bodies will receive immortality and incorruptibility from the Father. As such, death, within the overall economy of God seen in the light of the Passion of Christ, takes on a eucharistic dimension, alongside its educative and limiting function, and the economy as a whole can be described as the eucharist of God.

In this way, then, without denying the catastrophic reality of human apostasy and death—that the creature brought into being by God to share in his own life and glory turned his back on his Creator and so ends up rotting in the grave—it is possible, nevertheless, to see the same reality embraced within the overarching economy of God, as a means of bringing his creation, made from mud, to the full maturity of a human being, made in the image and likeness of God, knowing both good and evil, but rejecting the evil by turning in repentance to God. This, at the same time, demonstrates the wisdom and the power of God, a power which is made perfect in weakness. This possibility is given by Christ's own Passion, opening up a theological vision which, retrospectively, infuses the whole of our human, and humanly created, condition, with the power of God, the power that he manifests on the cross. Finally, the goal of this whole economy is to bring about an accurate knowledge, as St Irenaeus put it, "of things as they are, that is, of God and the human being." The truth about God revealed in, through, and as Christ, the crucified and exalted Lord, coincides with the truth about human beings. Only by having a proper comprehension of reality—the truth about God and about human beings—can we become that which God has called us to be.

"BEHOLD THE MAN!"

Having searched the scriptures in the light of Christ to understand how and why we were brought into being, we can now return to the Gospel of John, to hear the words of Christ from the cross with a fuller comprehension. When Christ said "It is finished" (Jn 19.30), he is not simply declaring that his earthly life has come to an end, but that rather the work of God is now "fulfilled" or "completed." The divine economy, that is, the whole plan of creation *and* salvation, told from this perspective, culminates at this point. The work of God spoken of in Genesis, creating "the human being [*anthrōpos*] in our image and likeness" (Gen 1.26–27), is completed here: as Pilate said a few verses earlier, "Behold, the man [*anthrōpos*]" (Jn 19.5). The work of God is complete, and the Lord of creation now rests from his work in the tomb on the blessed Sabbath. By himself undergoing the Passion as a man, Jesus Christ, as Son of God and himself God, fashions us *into* the image and likeness of God, the image of God that he himself *is* (Col 1.15).

According to the apostle Paul, the preaching of the gospel is to continue, building up the Church, "until we all attain to the unity of the faith and the knowledge of the Son of God, to mature manhood, to the measure of the stature of the fullness of Christ" (Eph 4.13). That Christ is the first true human being, and that we ourselves only become fully human in his stature, is a point made by many Christian writers across the centuries. As the Letter of Barnabas puts it, "It is concerning us that the scripture says that he says to the Son, 'Let us make man after our image and likeness.' "[44] More dramatically, St Ignatius of Antioch implores the Christians at Rome not to interfere with his coming martyrdom:

> It is better for me to die in Christ Jesus than to be king over the ends of the earth. I seek him who died for our sake. I desire him who rose for us. The pains of birth are upon me. Suffer me, my brethren; hinder me not from living, do not wish me to die. Do not give to the world one who desires to belong to God, nor deceive him with material things. Suffer me to receive the pure light; when I shall have arrived there, I shall become a human being [*anthrōpos*]. Suffer me to follow the example of the passion of my God.[45]

For St Ignatius, undergoing death in witness to Christ—the "perfect human being" or the "new human being"[46]—is a birth into a new life, to emerge as Christ himself, a fully human being. For St Ignatius, moreover, there is a connection between the Passion of Christ and his title "Word of God," such that this title is one shared by those who confess Christ in martyrdom. Again beseeching the Romans not to speak on his behalf before the authorities, but rather to keep silent, he states that "if you are silent concerning me, I am a word of God; but if you love my flesh, I shall be only a cry."[47] By undergoing the same martyr's death as Christ, the suffering God, he hopes to attain to the true light, to true humanity after the stature of Christ, and so to be a word of God, rather than only an inarticulate cry.

For St Irenaeus, whose theological vision has guided much of this chapter, "the work of God is the fashioning of the human being [*anthrōpos*]."[48] When he asserts that "the glory of God is the living human being,"[49] this is not simply an endorsement of what we might now think it is to be "fully alive" in this world. Rather, for St Irenaeus, the "living human being" is the martyr, going to death in confession of Christ:

> In this way, therefore, the martyrs bear witness and despise death: not after the weakness of the flesh, but by the readiness of the Spirit. For when the weakness of the flesh is absorbed, it manifests the Spirit as powerful; and again, when the Spirit absorbs the weakness, it inherits the flesh for itself, and from both of these is made a living human being: living, indeed, because of the participation of the Spirit; and human, because of the substance of the flesh.[50]

The strength of God is made perfect in weakness, and so, paradoxically, it is in their death, their ultimate vulnerability, that the martyrs bear greatest witness to the strength of God. Not that they reckon death to be a thing of no importance, but that in their confession they are vivified by the Spirit, living the life of the Spirit, who absorbs the weakness of their flesh into his own strength. When the Spirit so possesses the flesh, the flesh itself adopts the quality of the Spirit and is rendered like the Word of God.[51] The paradigm of the living human being is Jesus Christ himself and those who follow in his footsteps, the martyrs, flesh vivified by the Spirit.

Five centuries later, St Maximus the Confessor similarly affirms that the man Jesus Christ "has fulfilled, in word and truth, with unchangeable obedience, everything that he, as God, has predetermined to take place, and has accomplished the whole will of God the Father on our behalf."[52] In the cosmic vision of St Maximus, Christ's work has removed all the divisions and separations which characterize our present experience of created reality, and which have resulted from the misuse of the power given to us for the purpose of uniting all in Christ. Among these is the distinction between males and females:

> First he united us in himself by removing the difference between male and female, and instead of men and women, in whom above all this manner of division is beheld, he showed us as properly and truly to be simply human beings [*anthrōpos*], thoroughly transfigured in accordance with him, and bearing his intact and completely unadulterated image.[53]

Following the apostle Paul (cf. Gal 3.28), St Maximus asserts that in Christ the distinction between male and female is removed. The removal of this distinction means that in Christ, and only in him, can we see both men and women as what they truly are: human beings.

This perspective is held throughout the Byzantine era. Nicholas Cabasilas, writing in the fourteenth century, also asserts that it is not Adam but Christ who is the first true human being in history:

> It was for the new human being [*anthrōpos*] that human nature was created at the beginning, and for him mind and desire were prepared. . . . It was not the old Adam who was the model for the new, but the new Adam for the old. . . . For those who have known him first, the old Adam is the archetype because of our fallen nature. But for him who sees all things before they exist, the first Adam is the imitation of the second. To sum it up: the Savior first and alone showed to us the true human being [*anthrōpos*], who is perfect on account of both character and life and in all other respects.[54]

Not only is Christ the first true human being, but he is the model in whose image Adam, "a type of the one to come" (Rom 5.14), was already created. As we have seen, this is something which we have yet to become: as history has unfolded, we first know the humanity of Adam, a life of apostasy and death, but this provides the framework and the means by which we are to grown into the stature of human nature as manifest in Christ himself.

Finally, an example from a Latin writer, who brings out one further aspect of this mystery. Combining the two accounts of the creation of the human being given in Genesis (Gen 1.26–7; 2.7), Tertullian focuses our attention on the body:

> Whatever [form] the clay expressed, in mind was Christ who was to become human (which the clay was) and the Word flesh (which the earth then was). For the Father had already said to his Son, "Let us make man unto our image and likeness; and God made man," that is the same as "fashioned" [cf. Gen 2.7], "unto the image of God made he him" [Gen 1.26–27]—it means of Christ. And the Word is also God, who "being in the form of God, thought it not robbery to be equal to God" [Phil 2.6]. Thus that clay, already putting on the image of Christ, who was to be in the flesh, was not only the work, but also the pledge of God.[55]

Our body is not only the handiwork of God, being fashioned into the image and likeness of God, that is, of Christ who is to come, but also the "pledge" of God that this indeed shall come to pass. In the body, then, this clay, the mystery of Christ is being wrought, and so in the body Christians are now to "glorify God" (1 Cor 6.20). But before we turn to consider this aspect of being human, we should turn first to look further at our birth into this reality.

NOTES

[1]This is noted by R. Williams, *Resurrection: Interpreting the Easter Gospel* (New York: Pilgrim Press, 1984), 34; a remarkable work, to which the following paragraphs are much indebted.

[2]*Resurrection*, 11.

[3]*Resurrection*, 40.

[4]St Ignatius of Antioch *Letter to the Ephesians* 20.

[5]St Irenaeus of Lyons *Against the Heresies* 3.22.3.

[6]As argued, for instance, by J. Meyendorff (*Byzantine Theology*, 2nd rev. edn. [New York: Fordham University Press, 1987], 143–46), though that it "makes sin inevitable" (p. 145) seems to undermine the very point being made. Moreover, reading *eph o* as meaning "because *of death*" makes the pronoun play too many roles: it cannot, together with the preposition, be a contraction, meaning "because," and also refer back to "death," to say that "because of death all men have sinned." The verse simply says that death has still spread to all *because* all have sinned. Cf. Ezek 18.4, "only the man that sins shall die." St John Chrysostom, in his seventeenth homily on First Corinthians (NPNF, series 1, vol. 12), argues extensively that one should not attribute sin to mortality.

[7]St Athanasius *Against the Pagans* 2–3. Ed. and trans., together with *On the Incarnation*, R. W. Thomson, OECT (Oxford: Clarendon Press, 1971).

[8]St Maximus the Confessor *Questions to Thalassius* 61. Ed. C. Laga and C. Steel, CCSG 22 (Turnhout: Brepols, 1990), 85; Eng. trans. in P. M. Blowers and R. L. Wilken, *On the Cosmic Mystery of Jesus Christ: Selected Writings from St Maximus the Confessor* (Crestwood, NY: St Vladimir's Seminary Press, 2003), 131.

[9]See James Barr, *The Garden of Eden and the Hope of Immortality* (Minneapolis, MN: Fortress Press, 1993), to which the following paragraphs are indebted.

[10]Cf. Mark S. Smith, *The Origins of Biblical Monotheism: Israel's Polytheistic Background and the Ugaritic Texts* (New York: Oxford University Press, 2001).

[11]Classically stated by E. P. Sanders, *Paul and Palestinian Judaism* (Philadelphia: Fortress Press, 1977), esp. 474–75.

[12]St Irenaeus *Against the Heresies* 3.22.3.

[13]St Athanasius *Against the Pagans* 1; see also the opening paragraphs of his *On the Incarnation.*

[14]*Against the Pagans* 2; for creation *ex nihilo*, see *On the Incarnation* 2–3.

[15]*Against the Pagans* 41.

[16]*On the Incarnation* 13.

[17]*Against the Pagans* 19.

[18]St Gregory of Nyssa *Eunomius* 35 [3], cited in Chapter One.

[19]The phrase *felix culpa* is from the hymn "Exsultet," traditionally ascribed to St Augustine but now generally ascribed to St Ambrose, and used at the lighting of the Paschal candle in the Latin tradition: "O truly necessary sin of Adam, which was blotted out by the death of Christ. / O happy guilt, which was meet to have such and so great a redeemer" [*O certe necessarium Adae peccatum: quod Christi morte deletum est. / O felix culpa: quae talem ac tantum meruit habere redemptorem.*] F. Brittain, ed. *The Penguin Book of Latin Verse* (Baltimore, MD: Penguin, 1962), 94.

[20]St Justin Martyr *First Apology* 55, 60. Ed. M. Marcovich, PTS 38 (Berlin and New York: De Gruyter, 1994); trans. in ANF 1.

[21]St Isaac of Syria "*The Second Part*" 11.3. Ed. and trans. S. Brock, CSCO 55, scrip. syr. 225 (Louvain: Peeters, 1995).

[22]Cf. T. Talley, *The Origins of the Liturgical Year*, 2nd rev. ed. (Collegeville, MN: Liturgical Press, 1991), 11.

[23]Origen *Commentary on the Gospel of John* 1.33. Ed. and French trans. C. Blanc, SC 290 (Paris: Cerf, 1982); Eng. trans. in R. E. Heine, FC 89 (Washington, D.C.: Catholic University of America Press, 1993).

[24]*Commentary on the Gospel of John* 19.28.

[25]St Irenaeus *Against the Heresies* 4.37.7.

[26]*Against the Heresies* 4.39.1.

[27]*Against the Heresies* 4.37.7.

[28]*Against the Heresies* 4.38.1.

[29]*Against the Heresies* 4.38.3.

[30]*Against the Heresies* 4.38.4; cf. 2 Cor 5.4; 1 Cor 15.53; Gen 1.26, 3.5, 3.22.

[31]St Ignatius of Antioch *Letter to the Ephesians* 20.

[32]See Kartsonis, *Anastasis*, 4–7 and passim, for many pertinent comments, though with caution.

[33]St Ignatius of Antioch *Letter to the Smyrneans* 7.

[34]St Athanasius *On the Incarnation* 27; see the whole section from 27 to 32.

[35]St John Climacus *Ladder of Divine Ascent* step 29. Trans. C. Luibheid and N. Russell, CWS (Ramsey, NJ: Paulist Press, 1982).

[36]Idiomelon hymn, by St John of Damascus, in the funeral service; Sticheron from the Aposticha, Friday Vespers, Octoechos, tone 8.

[37]St Irenaeus *Against the Heresies* 3.20.1.

[38]Cf. *Against the Heresies* 3.23.5; 4.pref.4.

[39]*Against the Heresies* 3.20.2.

[40]Theophilus of Antioch *To Autolycus* 2.25–26. Ed. and trans. R. M. Grant, OECT (Oxford: Clarendon Press, 1970).

[41]St Gregory of Nyssa *The Great Catechism* 8. Ed. E. Mühlenberg, GNO 3.4 (Leiden: Brill, 1996), 31; Eng. trans. in NPNF, series 2, vol. 5.

[42]St Ignatius *Letter to the Romans* 4.

[43]*Against the Heresies* 5.2.3.

[44]*The Letter of Barnabas* 6.12. Ed. and trans. K. Lake, LCL The Apostolic Fathers 1 (Cambridge, MA: Harvard University Press, 1985 [1912]).

[45]St Ignatius *Letter to the Romans* 6.

[46]St Ignatius *Letter to the Smyrnaeans* 4.2; *Letter to the Ephesians* 20.1.

[47]St Ignatius *Letter to the Romans* 2.1.

[48]St Irenaeus *Against the Heresies* 5.15.2.

[49]*Against the Heresies* 4.20.7.

[50]*Against the Heresies* 5.9.2.

[51]*Against the Heresies* 5.9.3.

[52]St Maximus the Confessor *Ambigua* 41. PG 91.1309d; trans. in A. Louth, *Maximus the Confessor*, The Early Church Fathers (New York and London: Routledge, 1996).

[53]*Ambigua* 41. PG 91.1309d-1312a.

[54]Nicholas Cabasilas, *The Life in Christ* 6.91–4. Ed. and French trans. M.-H. Congourdeau, SC 361 (Paris: Cerf, 1990); Eng. trans. C. J. deCatanzaro (Crestwood, NY: St Vladimir's Seminary Press, 1974), where it is numbered as 6.12.

[55]Tertullian *On the Resurrection of the Flesh* 6. Ed. and trans. E. Evans (London: SPCK, 1960); modifying the translation of Evans.

CHAPTER FOUR

The Virgin Mother

From the beginning, the gospel of the crucified and exalted Lord was proclaimed in terms of a birth, both that of Christ and of Christians. The letters of the apostle Paul, which, it should be remembered, predate the writing of the four canonical Gospels, do not even mention the name of Mary, though they do mention that Christ "was born of a woman, born under the law" (Gal 4.4) and that Christ is of the line of David (Rom 1.3). However, the apostle does use the language of hearing and receiving the Word, to describe the begetting of Christ, that is later used of Mary in the infancy narratives, and uses it to great effect. Having preached the gospel—that Christ died and rose according to scripture—giving birth to faith in Christ, a faith which comes from hearing (Rom 10.17), the apostle has the task of nourishing the new Christians. He writes to the Thessalonians in very tender terms:

> We were gentle among you, like a nurse taking care of her children. So, being affectionately desirous of you, we were ready to share with you not only the gospel of God, but also our own selves, because you had become dear to us. (1 Thess 2.7–8)

Then he continues:

> You know how, like a father with his children, we exhorted each one of you and encouraged and charged you to lead a life worthy of God, who calls you into his own kingdom and glory. (1 Thess 2.11–12)

He is not only their nurse, but also their father. In return, the Thessalonians are praised for receiving the apostle's preaching not "as the word of men but," he says, "as what it really is, the Word of God, which is at work in you believers" (1 Thess 2.13). Their faithful receptivity is a condition for receiving the apostle's message as the Word of God that it truly is.

Going one step further, while the apostle Paul likens himself in this way to one who nourishes his converts' faith, he also describes himself directly as the one who begot his readers. In his first epistle to the Corinthians, he writes:

> I do not write this to make you ashamed, but to admonish you as my beloved children. For though you have countless guides in Christ, you do not have many fathers. For I begot you in Christ Jesus through the gospel. (1 Cor 4.14–15)

Addressing the Galatians in even more dramatic terms, he speaks of himself as a mother giving birth to Christ: "My little children, with whom I am again in travail, until Christ be formed in you!" (Gal 4.19).

Christians are those who have been born again in Christ Jesus through the gospel; they are the ones who are having Christ formed in them. Finally, the apostle is not only the one who is in travail with them, but is the paradigm of the state to which they are called:

> I have been crucified with Christ: It is no longer I who live, but Christ who lives in me; and the life I now live in the flesh I live by faith in the Son of God, who loved me and gave himself for me. (Gal 2.20)

Having died to the flesh, Christ not only now lives in the apostle, but Paul no longer lives—he identifies himself with Christ. Writing to the Galatians, he speaks of God having "revealed his Son in me" (1.16, not "to" me, as RSV), and praises them for having received him "as an angel of God, as Christ Jesus" (4.14).

Born again through the gospel in Christ Jesus, Christians are the body of Christ. This is no loose analogy or metaphor; the apostle Paul makes the identification without qualification: "You are the body of Christ and individually members of it," all, that is, who "by the one Spirit were baptized into the one body" (1 Cor 12.27, 13). Christians are called to be "the one body" by living in subjection to the head, Christ, allowing his peace to rule in their hearts (Col 3.15). As members of his body, they depend for their life and being upon their head. As "firstborn of the dead," in whom "the whole fullness of divinity dwells bodily," Christ is "the head of the body, the Church" (Col 1.18–19, 2.9). It is by holding fast to the head that "the whole body, nourished and knit together through its joints and ligaments, grows with a growth that is from God" (Col 2.19). Christians also depend upon one another: "We, though many, are one body in Christ, and individually members of one another" (Rom 12.5). The grace given to each is for the benefit of the one body, so that everything is to be done in love for the building up of the one body (1 Cor 12–13).

Finally, the body of Christ is, as already mentioned, the Church: Christ has been made "the head over all things for the Church, which is his body, the fullness of him who fills all in all" (Eph 1.22–3). The "profound mystery" of the man leaving his parents and joining to his wife, becoming one flesh (Gen 2.24), refers, according to the apostle Paul, "to Christ and the Church" (Eph 5.32). Writing to the Corinthians, the apostle says that he has betrothed them to Christ, that he might "present [them] as a pure virgin to her one husband," though he fears that they will be led astray from their pure devotion by those who preach another Jesus or a different gospel (1 Cor 11.2–4). The proclamation of the gospel is clearly understood by the apostle in terms of giving birth to Christians, those who respond to the Word of the Cross, the Word of God, in faith. He is in travail with them, forming Christ in them, in those, that is, who are both individually and collectively the body of Christ. It brings Christians into a new relationship with God, whereby, sharing in the Spirit bestowed in the risen Christ, they also can call upon God as "abba, Father" (Rom 8.15; Gal 4.6).

In all of this, the apostle, and those who followed him, were following the movement of a scriptural passage that we looked at in Chapter One—the "fourth hymn of the Suffering Servant" (Is 52.13–53.12), which speaks of the suffering of the servant, bruised for our iniquities and pouring out his soul unto death. This passage is read, in the Orthodox tradition, only at vespers on Holy Friday afternoon. Having read the Passion Gospels at Holy Friday Matins (often served on Thursday evening), standing at the foot of the cross placed in the middle of the church, the service of vespers then includes the celebration of the "Rite of Entombment": reenacting how Joseph of Arimathea took down the body of Christ from the cross and placed it in the new-hewn tomb, where no one had ever been laid (cf. Lk 23.53 and the parallel verses Mt 27:60 and Jn 19:41). It is at this point in the service that the "fourth hymn of the Suffering Servant" is read. But, while this hymn is usually reckoned to finish at chapter 53.12, the prescribed reading includes the following verse:

> Sing, O barren one, who did not bear; break forth into singing and cry aloud, you who have not been in travail! For the children of the desolate one will be more than the children of her that is married, says the Lord. (Is 54.1)

While modern scholarship asserts that this begins the next oracle, within the tradition of the Orthodox church, the proclamation of the Suffering Servant concludes with the joyful exclamation that the barren one will give birth. For it is, after all, into Christ's death and resurrection that Christians are baptized, being born again of the water and the Spirit, putting on Christ, and living in him by the grace of the Spirit as sons of God (Rom 6ff). The effect of this passage from Isaiah must have been all the more vivid when, as used to be the custom, Easter was the time for the baptism of those who had received their final catechizing during the forty days of Great Lent.

THE CHURCH AS VIRGIN MOTHER

Given all of this scriptural imagery, it is not surprising that Christians, from the earliest times onwards, have spoken of the Church as their Mother, or the Virgin Mother. One of the most extensive of such reflections comes from one of the most unusual texts of the second century, *The Shepherd of Hermas*, which was counted as scripture by some and included in the Codex Sinaiticus, following the New Testament. The first section of the work describes various visions, in which a woman appears to Hermas, a woman who is identified as the Church. In the first vision, in which she chides Hermas for his sin of desiring his mistress as a wife, she appears as an old woman, "clothed in shining garments and holding a book in her hand."[1] After his second vision, Hermas has another:

> And a revelation was made to me, brethren, while I slept, by a very beautiful young man, who said to me, "Who do you think that the ancient lady was from whom you received the little book?" I said, "The Sibyl." "You are wrong," he said, "she is not." "Who is she, then?" I said. "The Church," he said. I said to him, "Why then is she old?" "Because," he said, "she was created the first of all things. For this reason she is old; and for her sake the world was established."[2]

In a later vision, the old woman shows Hermas a tower being built out of stones that had been prepared for the task. The stones that were cracked, rotten, or the wrong shape were rejected, while the stones that were used fitted together so well that the tower seemed to be built out of one stone. When he asked for an explanation, Hermas was told by the woman: "The tower which you see being built is myself, the Church, who has appeared to you both now and formerly."[3] There then follows a long allegory of the tower and the stones, after which she addresses the Christians of Rome:

> Listen to me, my children! It is I who have brought you up in all simplicity, innocence and holiness by the mercy of the Lord; it is I who have caused justice to fall on you, drop by drop. . . . Listen to me and make peace among yourselves . . . so that, standing joyfully before the Father, I can render him a favorable account of you.[4]

The Church is personified as a female figure, not so much in terms of a mother giving birth (this is absent in Hermas, as is any allusion to the Pauline theology considered earlier), but as a mother who nourishes her children, preparing them to become the building of the Church, which is herself. This formative process is paralleled by the changing appearance of the woman in successive visions: she begins as an old woman, older than all creation, and then in each successive vision, she appears younger every time, until, in the fourth vision, she appears as a maiden " 'adorned as if coming forth from the bridal chamber' [Ps 19.5], all in white and with white sandals, veiled to her forehead, and a turban for a head-dress, but her hair was white."[5] The Church is at once older than the rest of creation; she is created first of all things, and all things are created for her. But as the revelation continues, she becomes a pure virgin, for it is as a spotless virgin that the apostle Paul says that he *will* present his communities to Christ: this is something to be achieved, something that lies in the future.

The idea that the Church preexists creation is also found in the *Second Epistle of Clement*: "Brethren, if we do the will of our Father God, we shall belong to the first Church, the spiritual one which was created before the sun and moon." The *Epistle* continues by interpreting the statement that "God made man male and female" as referring to Christ and the Church and claims that

> the books and the Apostles declare that the Church belongs not to the present, but has existed from the beginning; for she was spiritual, as also was our Jesus, but was made manifest in the last days that he [or more likely: she] might save us; and the Church, which is spiritual, was made manifest in the flesh of Christ, showing us that if any one of us guard her in the flesh without corruption, he shall receive back again in the Holy Spirit.[6]

The manifestation of Jesus is also the manifestation of the Church, his body, which is to be preserved in the flesh in purity, so that those belonging to the Church might receive the Spirit—that is, become truly spiritual.

In another text from the late second century, the Church is simply spoken of as the Virgin Mother. This is *The Letter of the Churches of Vienne and Lyons*, which describes in graphic detail the sufferings of the Christians of Gaul during the persecutions around the year AD 177.[7] During the first round in the arena, some of the Christians "appeared to be unprepared and untrained, as yet weak and unable to endure such a great conflict." About ten of these, the letter says, proved to be "stillborn" or "miscarried," causing great sorrow to the others and weakening the resolve of those yet to undergo their torture.[8] However, these stillborn Christians were encouraged through the zeal of the others, especially the slave girl Blandina, the heroine of the story, who was hung on a stake to be devoured by the wild beasts, but who appeared to the other Christians as the embodiment of Christ: "in their agony they saw with their outward eyes in the person of their sister the One who was crucified for them."[9]

After describing her suffering, and that of another Christian called Attalus, the letter continues:

> Through their continued life the dead were made alive, and the witnesses (martyrs) showed favor to those who had failed to witness. And there was great joy for the Virgin Mother in receiving back alive

> those who she had miscarried as dead. For through them the majority of those who had denied were again brought to birth and again conceived and again brought to life and learned to confess; and now living and strengthened, they went to the judgment seat.[10]

The Christians who turned away from making their confession are simply dead; their lack of preparation has meant that they are stillborn children of the Virgin Mother, the Church. But strengthened by the witness of others, they also are able to go to their death, and so the Virgin Mother receives them back alive—finally giving birth to living children of God. The death of the martyr, the letter says later on, is their "new birth" and is celebrated as their true birthday.[11]

It is possible that the *Letter of the Martyrs of Vienne and Lyons* was written by St Irenaeus, who succeeded Pothinus as bishop of Lyons, when Pothinus died during the persecutions. St Irenaeus also speaks of the new birth granted by the Virgin. Criticizing the Ebionites, those who claim that Christ was born of a woman just as any other human being is born, St Irenaeus asks:

> How can they be saved, unless it was God who wrought out their salvation upon earth? Or how shall the human being arrive at God, unless God has first come to human beings? And how shall he escape from the generation subject to death, if not by means of a new generation, given in a wonderful manner by God as a sign of salvation—that regeneration which flows from the Virgin through faith.[12]

Given the context of a debate with the Ebionites, the reference to the Virgin here is certainly to Mary—the new birth manifested by Christ's own arrival in this world. But it is no less a new birth for all Christians, who by faith are reborn in the virginal womb of the Church.

The same identification is made by St Irenaeus a little later in the same chapter:

> There are those who say that "He is a man, and who shall know him?" [Jer 17.9]; and, "I came unto the prophetess, and she bore a son, and his name is called Wonderful Counselor, the Mighty God" [Is 8.3, 9.6]; and those who proclaimed the Immanuel, born of the Virgin [Is 7.14]: declaring the union of the Word of God with his own handiwork, that the Word would become flesh, and the Son of God the Son of man—the pure one opening purely that pure womb which regenerates human beings unto God and which he himself made pure, having become that which we are, he is "God Almighty" and has a generation which cannot be declared.[13]

Christ, becoming human, as prophesied by Isaiah, opens the pure womb—the womb by which we are also regenerated unto God.

One of the most unusual examples of using the term "Virgin" to refer to the Church comes from Clement of Alexandria, writing again at the end of the second century. For Clement, the Virgin is not only our mother, giving us birth into the life of God, but is also the one who supplies nourishment to her infants:

> The Lord Jesus, fruit of the Virgin, did not proclaim women's breasts to be blessed, nor did he choose them to give nourishment. But when the Father, full of goodness and love for men, rained down his Word upon the earth, this same Word became the spiritual nourishment for virtuous men. O mysterious marvel!
>
> There is one Father of all, there is one Word of all, and the Holy Spirit is one and the same everywhere. There is also one Virgin Mother, whom I love to call the Church. Alone, this mother had no milk because she alone did not become a woman. She is virgin and mother simultaneously, a virgin undefiled and a mother full of love. She draws her children to herself and nurses them with holy milk, that is, the Word for infants. She had not milk because the milk was this child, beautiful and familiar, the body of Christ.[14]

The fruit of the Virgin here is Christ, not simply, however, as the one to whom she gives birth, but as her milk, the milk by which she nourishes those for whom she is mother. Again there is the suggestion that the Church already existed, a virgin waiting to become a mother while yet preserving her virginity. It is possible that the image of milk has eucharistic overtones, for there were Christians who used milk, sometimes with honey, in their ritual meals, often connected with baptism.[15]

That the mother preserves her virginity is stated explicitly, for the first time, by Clement of Alexandria. He affirms the perpetual virginity of Mary by a very intriguing comparison:

> It appears that even today many hold that Mary, after the birth of her Son, was found to be in the state of a woman who has given birth, while in fact she was not so. For some say that, after giving birth, she was examined by a midwife, who found her to be a virgin. Now such to us are the scriptures of the Lord, which gave birth to the truth and remain virgin, in the hiddenness of the mysteries of truth. "She gave birth and did not give birth," scripture says, since she conceives by herself, not by conjunction.[16]

Mary remained a virgin, just as the scriptures give birth to the truth while remaining virginal. The proclamation of the gospel according to the scriptures results, as we have seen, in the birth of Christians to new life; yet this proclamation does not impair the purity and integrity of the scriptures. This connection between the truth conceived in the scriptures and Mary giving birth to her Son is one to which we will return at the end of this chapter.

Although Hermas and Irenaeus were writing in the West, they both wrote in Greek. In the Latin Church of this period, we can also see the same reflection on the Church as the Virgin Mother. This can be seen in pictorial form, for instance, in the magnificent frescoes of the Roman catacombs, especially the portrayal of the Virgin in the "orans" posture, with arms outstretched in the position for prayer, sometimes with the figure of the Christ child on her lap (cf. Plate 4), an image which continued to develop and be very popular in Byzantine and Russian iconography. Tertullian, writing in Carthage in the early third century, often speaks of the Church as Mother. On occasion, he also introduces into this imagery the figure of Eve. For example:

> As Adam was a figure of Christ, Adam's sleep shadowed out the death of Christ, who was to sleep a mortal slumber, that from the wound inflicted on his side might be figured the true Mother of the living, the Church.[17]

The Church, which came from the side of the crucified Christ (referring to the blood and the water, cf. Jn 19.34), is foreshadowed by the formation of Eve from the side of Adam when he was asleep, the sleep which foreshadowed Christ's own sleep in death. Thus, while Eve was certainly called the mother of the living (Gen 3.20), it is really the Church that is this.

St Cyprian, in the middle of the third century, also frequently speaks of the Church simply as Mother:

> She spreads her branches in generous growth over all the earth, she extends her abundant streams ever further; yet one is the head-spring, one the source, one the Mother who is prolific in her offspring, generation after generation: of her womb are we born, of her milk are we fed, from her Spirit our souls draw their life-breath. The spouse of Christ cannot be defiled, she is inviolate and chaste; she knows one home alone, in all modesty she keeps faithfully to one chamber. It is she who seals for the kingdom the sons whom she has borne. Whoever breaks with the Church and enters on an adulterous union, cuts himself off from the promises made to the Church. . . . You cannot have God for your Father if you no longer have the Church for your mother.[18]

For Cyprian the reality is such a given, that he simply speaks of the Church as Mother.

It is possible that the image of the Church as the Virgin also works in reverse. According to Epiphanius, Marcion, the first great heretic, was apparently thrown out of his father's church for violating a virgin.[19] It is possible that the reference here is not to a particular young woman, but to the Church herself: he has seduced those whom the apostle wants to present as a pure virgin to her one husband, by seducing Christians away from Christ by preaching another Jesus or another gospel (1 Cor 11.2–4).

These examples, all drawn from the first three centuries, make it clear that speaking of the Virgin, or the Virgin Mother, was a usual way of speaking of the Church. This language continued thereafter and is still found in Orthodox hymnography. For example, the troparion for the Resurrection in tone six proclaims:

> Angelic Powers were at your grave,
> and those who guarded it became as dead,
> and Mary stood by the tomb, seeking your most
> pure Body.
> You despoiled Hell and emerged unscathed;
> you met the Virgin and granted life.
> Lord, risen from the dead, glory to you![20]

Mary here is clearly Mary Magdalene and, just as clearly, "the Virgin" is not! Rather, given what we have seen, the Virgin to whom the risen Christ comes granting life is the Church, the Virgin who now becomes a virginal mother, granting new life to her children.

MARY AS A SYMBOL OF THE CHURCH

A notable feature of Orthodox Marian devotion is that at three of the four main feasts of Mary, the Virgin and Theotokos or "God-bearer"—the feasts for her Nativity, her Entry into the Temple, and her Dormition (the exception being the feast of the Annunciation, the only event described in the canonical Gospels)—the gospel reading prescribed for the Liturgy is the passage from Luke (10.38–42), which contrasts Martha's busy service with Mary's sitting still at Jesus' feet and hearing his Word; but the reading then concludes with a verse taken from halfway through the following chapter, where Jesus addresses the crowd with these words:

> As he spoke these things, a certain woman of the company lifted up her voice and said to him: "Blessed is the womb that bore you, and the breasts that you sucked." But he said, "Blessed rather are those that hear the Word of God and keep it." (Lk 11.27–28)

Christ's words are striking precisely because they direct our attention away from his biological mother—the womb that bore him and the breasts that he sucked—and focus our attention instead on the condition of faith—hearing the Word and keeping it: as Christ says earlier in the same Gospel, when told that his mother and brothers standing outside want to see him, "My mother and my brothers are those who hear the Word of God and do it" (Lk 8.21). Those who hear the Word of God, receiving the Word and embodying it, giving it flesh, are, in Christ's own words, his mother and brother.

Yet, at the same time, the Gospels present no one else as keeping the Word of God in a pure heart apart from Mary, the Mother of Jesus. This is what we celebrate in the Feast of the Annunciation: that Mary, as she is presented in the infancy narratives of the Gospels of Matthew and Luke, hears the Word of God announced by the angel, accepts it, and conceives Christ in her womb. As she herself embodies in this event the receptivity to the Word spoken of by Christ, the saying of Christ read at the other Marian feasts ("blessed rather are those that hear the Word of God and keep it") is not read this time.

One other episode in the canonical Gospels, in fact its climactic event, presents Mary's faithfulness to the Word and her adherence to Christ: the Crucifixion, as described in the Gospel according to John. In the Synoptic Gospels, Mary is not present: the disciples had abandoned Christ (or even, as Peter, denied him), while the women who had ministered to him stood some distance apart: Mary Magdalene, Mary the mother of James and Joseph, and the mother of the sons of Zebedee (Mt 27.56; Mk 15.41; Lk 23.49 just mentions the women from Galilee standing at a distance). But in the Gospel of John, we have the scene thereafter depicted in Byzantine iconography: Jesus on the cross, with his mother and the beloved disciple standing at its foot (the Gospel also mentions his mother's sister, Mary, the wife of Cleopas, and Mary Magdalene—but they recede into the background on the icon, if they are there at all). The words spoken by Christ from the cross pertain, once again, to motherhood: "Woman behold your son"; and to the disciple, "Behold your mother" (Jn 19.26–27).

It is not simply that the Gospel of John reports details of which the other evangelists were ignorant or had forgotten. What we have in the Gospel of John, the theological Gospel *par excellence*, is already a theological interpretation of the event of the Passion, in terms of the fertile preaching of the gospel. By Christ's own words, his mother is now the mother of the beloved disciple, and this disciple is himself identified with Christ: as Origen points out, Christ does not say, "Woman behold another son for you in my place," but "behold your son," or, as Origen paraphrases it, "this is Jesus whom you bore."[21] Those who stand by the cross, and are not ashamed of it, receive as their mother the one who embodies this fertile, generative, faithfulness, and they themselves become sons of God, for they have Christ, the Son of God, living in them.

In the infancy narratives of the Gospels of Matthew and Luke, and in the Passion as it is presented in the Gospel of John, and, following them, in the celebration of the Annunciation and the Crucifixion, we look on Mary as the one who is obedient to God, enabling the birth of the Son of God and opening the way for others to become sons of God. Elsewhere in the Gospels, however, Mary is not portrayed as the embodiment of this virtue: she searches anxiously for her young son, and is astonished to find him in his Father's house debating with the teachers (Lk 2.41–51); when Jesus was rumored to be "besides himself," "possessed by Beelzebub," his mother and his brothers went "to seize him" but were told in return that "whoever does the will of God is my brother, and sister, and mother" (Mk 3.21–35); and, when Mary makes her request at the marriage celebration in Cana, she receives a sharp rebuke from Christ: "O woman, what have you to do with me? My hour has not yet come!" (Jn 2.4, as in RSV. Literally, "what [is there between] you and me"). St John Chrysostom picks up on these two aspects of the presentation of Jesus' mother in the Gospels. Commenting on the words of Christ about his mother and his brothers, he describes Mary as being a demanding mother, overconfident in her authority over her son, "not yet thinking," as Chrysostom says, "anything great about him." His conclusion is that "we learn here that even to have borne Christ in the womb, and to have brought forth that marvelous birth, has no profit, if there is not virtue." But, he continues, Christ "has pointed out a spacious road: and it is granted not only to women but also to men, to be of this rank, or rather of one yet higher. For this makes one his mother much more than those pangs did."[22]

This latter image of Mary does not sit well with much popular Marian piety (though St John Chrysostom was not averse to it). But rather than avoiding the image of Mary that it presents, we should consider them both together and, more specifically, *how* Mary is spoken of in each, to be led more fully into the mystery of Christ. As we have seen in the preceding chapters, how we view Christ, the scriptures, and the whole of creation and its history, depends on our first principle, our hypothesis. Such also is the case for Mary: the two images presented of her in the New Testament depend on two different ways of speaking about her. In one, what has been called a "dynamic view," "Mary starts off, as it were, in the position to which Eve had reduced the human race," so that it is through Christ alone that we are brought back into paradise, for his work re-creates all of creation and its history. This enables us to see Mary as the New Eve and is the starting point for the second way of speaking about Mary, a "static view": beginning with Mary as the New Eve, the one who by her obedience to God conceived and gave flesh to the Word, it now regards "Mary's position as having been *throughout* her life that of Eve *before* the Fall."[23]

Theologically and historically, the first way of speaking about Mary is primary: Christ alone is the mediator, redeemer, and savior. But as *theology* always speaks in the light of the risen Christ, a light which illumines and transfigures all of creation and its history, most Fathers tend to speak of Mary in term of Eve before the Fall (Chrysostom's comments, mentioned earlier, are an exception). Because of this, great caution is needed when reading what they say about Mary, lest what is said of Mary theologically, in the light of Christ's work, is taken as being said as a modern historical affirmation, as a description of her life prior to, and thus independent of, Christ.

The theological task of seeing Mary in the light of the work of Christ continued, with varying degrees of success, in the various apocryphal texts concerning Mary, and in those elements that were picked up, or independently developed, in the other liturgical Marian feasts—her Nativity, her Entry into the Temple, and her Dormition. As we will see, the Annunciation and conception of Christ is intimately related to the Passion of Christ and the proclamation of the gospel, and when the other Marian feasts come to be celebrated, they are always described in terms of what has happened in and through Christ, even to the point of Thomas again being late for her Dormition. These Marian feasts present a theological reflection on who Mary is and what she has done, made in the light of Christ's work of salvation: they are a confessional statement of faith, a theological reflection based upon Christ. In the scriptural descriptions of the Annunciation and the Nativity of Christ, and in the other liturgical celebrations of Mary, we are directed not to Mary herself, but to Mary as the one who received the Word and gave birth to Christ, and whose whole life is transfigured by this, and we are given all this as an exhortation for us also to receive the Word, standing firmly by the cross and putting on the identity of Christ.

This way of viewing Mary, in the light of the work of Christ, brings her into a close relationship with the Church. This connection is not usually made explicit in the writings from the first three centuries, the infancy narratives of Matthew and Luke, and the Passion as it is described in the Gospel of John being the most important exceptions. In this period, the typology most usually employed to describe Mary is that of Eve, contrasting the disobedient virgin to the obedient virgin. The Church, on the other hand, as we have seen, is frequently personified, as a woman, a Virgin, or Virgin Mother, in whom we have received our new birth, or, following the apostle Paul, the birth of Christ in us. But from the fourth century onwards, Mary is brought into this reflection about the Church, frequently in a quite surprising manner, but one that can help us understand how Mary is presented in the "infancy narratives" of Matthew and Luke, and why she is present at the Passion in the Gospel of John.

St Ephrem the Syrian, whose poetic writings lend themselves most readily to such associations of images, develops this point extensively. For example:

> The Virgin Mary is a symbol of the Church, when she receives the first announcement of the gospel. And, it is in the name of the Church that Mary sees the risen Jesus. Blessed be God, who filled Mary and the Church with joy. We call the Church by the name of Mary, for she deserves a double name.[24]

At first glance, St Ephrem seems confused: he identifies the Mary that saw the risen Jesus (i.e., Mary Magdalene, according to the Gospels) with Mary, the mother of Jesus. But he has not simply mixed up the accounts given in the Gospels. He is not merely interpreting the texts of the Gospels in themselves, in a modern manner, but rather unfolding the mystery of Christ that they present. His identification is based on the fact that both Marys received the gospel—first as an annunciation, and then by seeing the risen Jesus.

There are two points of importance here. First, it is *when* she receives the proclamation of the gospel that she is seen as Mary, and not at the other moments when she appears in the narratives: "Mary" here is the one who receives the proclamation of the gospel, and so both "Marys" can be identified. Second, viewed in this way, she is a symbol of the Church, not the other way around: Mary is not the archetype of the Church, but the symbol of the Church. The Church, we should recall, is thought of as being older than all creation; Mary, as the one who receives the gospel, is a "symbol of the Church" and is described as such in the infancy narratives and the Passion narrative in the Gospel of John. As we have seen, such reflection begins by considering how the fertile, generative preaching of the gospel is received, and leads to the understanding of the Church as Mother or Virgin Mother, and then links the Church with her symbol, Mary. So strong is this connection between the Church and her symbol, Mary (when seen in this light), that St Ephrem can simply call the Church "Mary." In doing so, he clearly follows along the theological lines already laid out in the infancy narratives and the Passion as presented in the Gospel of John, and in return helps us understand why and how it is that Mary is presented in this distinctive manner in these places.

A similar point is made by St Ephrem in another hymn, where he identifies Mary and the Church on the grounds that they both recognize the risen Christ:

> Three angels were seen at the tomb:
> these three announced that he was risen on the third day.
> Mary, who saw him, is the symbol of the Church
> which will be the first to recognize the signs of his second
> coming.[25]

The Church is the one who will first recognize the coming Lord, and so Mary (again conflating the two Marys), as the one who, in the resurrection accounts, first encounters the risen Christ, is the symbol of the Church—the Church that awaits the return of Christ, looking towards the heavens, where Christians have their citizenship, for "from it we await our Savior, the Lord Jesus Christ, who will change our lowly body to be like his glorious body" (Phil 3.20–21), so that "when he appears, we shall be like him" (1 Jn 3.2).

St Ephrem also identifies the Church with Mary on the basis of the words of Jesus from the cross to the beloved disciple. Commenting on the words of those who were fed in the wilderness, "this is the prophet concerning whom it was said that he would come into the world" (Jn 6.14), St Ephrem points to the parallel between Christ and Moses:

> They were repeating that [word] of Moses, "the Lord will raise up a prophet for you," not an ordinary one, but one "like me" [Deut 18.15], who will feed you bread in the desert. "Like me," he walked on the sea [cf. Mt 14.25–31] and appeared in the cloud [cf. Mt 17.5]. He freed his Church from the circumcision, and established John, who was a virgin, in place of Joshua, son of Nun. He confided Mary, his Church, to him [cf. Jn 19.25–7], as Moses [confided] his flock to Joshua, so that this [word], "like me," might be fulfilled.[26]

The Church, Mary, is entrusted to John, whom, St Ephrem notes, is also a virgin—one who has preserved his integrity, most importantly the purity of faith and the depth of theology (John is *the* theologian).

A final point of identification between Mary and the Church lies, for St Ephrem, in the way in which they both offer believers the true bread of life:

> The Church gave us the living Bread,
> in place of the unleavened bread that Egypt had given.
> Mary gave us the refreshing bread,
> in place of the fatiguing bread that Eve had procured for us.[27]

The Church and Mary are once again identified, as both giving us living and nourishing bread, in contrast to the food given in Egypt and the bread of toil procured by Eve. The relation between the Church and Mary was explored by many other writers in the fourth century, East and West, and thereafter, but for our present needs, St Ephrem has given us more than enough food for thought.

TOMB AND WOMB: THE MYSTERY OF THE INCARNATION

Having explored the reflection of the Fathers from the first four centuries on the Church as the Virgin, who by the preaching of the gospel has given birth to sons, and how Mary, as presented in the Annunciation and at the Crucifixion and Resurrection, was understood as a "symbol of the Church," we can now turn to a final aspect of the mysterious relation between Mary and the Church, and that is the connection between the tomb of Christ and the womb of Mary. As St Ephrem puts it:

> By your resurrection you convinced them
> about your birth, for the den was sealed
> and the grave was secured—the pure one in the den
> and the living one in the grave. Your witnesses were
> the sealed den and the grave.
> The womb and Sheol shouted with joy and cried out
> about your resurrection. The womb that was sealed

> conceived you; Sheol that was secured,
> brought you forth. Against nature
> the womb conceived and Sheol yielded.
> Sealed was the grave which they entrusted
> with keeping the dead man. Virginal was the womb
> that no man knew. The virginal womb
> and the sealed grave like trumpets
> for a deaf people, shouted in its ear.[28]

The virginal womb is correlated to the sealed tomb, for both proclaim the mystery of the risen Christ.

This connection between the tomb and the womb seems to have been behind the calculation for the date of the celebration of the Nativity of Christ. The Nativity of Christ only began to be celebrated in the East in the late fourth century, and thereafter it is explained in terms of solar symbolism, as a replacement of the pagan feast of the birth of the invincible sun.[29] Before any such considerations arose, however, the feast was celebrated in the West, where the date of 25 December was based on the date of the Passion, for this was reckoned to have occurred, nine months earlier, on 25 March (the Roman equivalent on the Julian calendar of the 14 Nissan on the Jewish calendar).[30] So in the liturgical calendar, the Passion of Christ was followed, nine months later, by the birth of Christ. Only subsequently was this date, counting now backwards from the Nativity, reckoned to be the date of Christ's conception.[31]

The connection between the tomb and the womb indicated by the dating of the feasts was still recognized at the time of St Augustine, who comments:

> He is believed to have been conceived on 25 March, and also to have suffered on that day. Thus to the new tomb he was buried in, where no mortal body was laid before or after, there corresponds the womb he was conceived in, where no mortal body was sown before or after.[32]

To the tomb corresponds the womb: the ordering here is significant, just as is the fact that Mary, as we have seen, is spoken of as a "symbol of the Church," not the other way round. We saw very clearly in the first chapter that Jesus Christ himself was known even by his disciples to be the Lord only after the Passion. Likewise, that Mary gave birth to the Word of God is known only after, and in the light of, the Passion, when the apostles reflect, by using scripture, on who it was that was crucified and risen: to the tomb corresponds the womb.

As such, the Mary that we are presented with in the infancy narratives (but not in the other places that she appears in the canonical Gospels) and at the Feast of Annunciation is already described in terms of the gospel of the crucified and risen Lord: the infancy narratives of Matthew and Luke are already told as a proclamation of the gospel (in the full sense), and Mary is presented here in the fullness of the theological vision made possible by the Passion.[33] This is also a connection made explicit in the icon for the Nativity (as in Plate 5 of this book, where it is combined, unusually but profoundly, with the Passion): in the icon, Christ is depicted, not in a house or stable (as a historicizing depiction of the infancy narratives would require), but wrapped in swaddling cloths as a corpse (with a cross in his halo), laid in a manger as food (for us who eat the body of Christ), and with the manger positioned in a cave embracing in its shape the Virgin, just as the crucified Christ was placed in a newly hewn (i.e., virgin) cave owned by the other Joseph. The same point can also be made by examining the liturgical hymnography of the Orthodox Church for the Feast of the Nativity, which is clearly based on that of Holy Week and the Passion.[34]

As Mary is known to have given birth to the Word of God only from the perspective of the Passion and exaltation of Christ, when seen and understood through the matrix of scripture, her conception and birth of Christ is already presented in these terms—to the tomb corresponds the womb. It is for this reason that Clement of Alexandria, as noted earlier, connects Christ's birth from the virginal womb with the virginal scriptures which give birth to the truth. In a passage from his treatise *On the Christ and the Antichrist*, Hippolytus of Rome brings together the Passion of Christ and the incarnation of the Word, woven from the fabric of scripture, through an extended metaphor:

> For the Word of God, being fleshless, put on the holy flesh from the holy Virgin, as a bridegroom a garment, having woven it for himself in the sufferings of the Cross, so that having mixed our mortal body with his own power, and having mingled the corruptible into the incorruptible, and the weak with the strong, he might save perishing man.
>
> The web-beam, therefore, is the passion of the Lord upon the cross;
> and the warp on it is the power of the Holy Spirit;
> and the woof is the holy flesh woven by the Spirit;
> and the thread is the grace which by the love of Christ binds and unites the two in one;
> and the rods are the Word;
> and the workers are the patriarchs and prophets who weave the fair, long, perfect tunic for Christ;
> and the Word passing through these, like the combs (or rods), completes through them that which his Father wills.[35]

The flesh of the Word, received from the Virgin and "woven in the sufferings of the Cross," is woven by the patriarchs and prophets, whose actions and words proclaim the manner in which the Word became present and manifest. That is, in the preaching of Jesus Christ—the proclamation of the one who died on the cross—interpreted and understood in the matrix, the womb, of scripture, the Word receives flesh from the Virgin. The Virgin in this case, Hippolytus later affirms following Revelation 12, is the Church, who will never cease "bearing from her heart the Word that is persecuted by the unbelieving in the world," while the male child she bears is Christ, God and man, announced by the prophets, "whom the Church continually bears as she teaches all nations."[36] The Virgin Church continually gives birth to Christ by her pure teaching, the gospel proclaimed according to scripture, so that the Word is made flesh in her children. Or, as St Maximus puts it, "Christ eternally wills to be born mystically, becoming incarnate through those who are saved and making the soul which begets him to be a virgin mother."[37]

That Mary gave birth to the Word of God is known after the Passion, when the apostles reflect, by using scripture, on who it was that was crucified and risen—it is a confessional statement, made in the light of the Passion and exaltation. The Mary thus presented to us in the infancy narratives and the Passion, as it is described in the Gospel of John—the Mary of Marian devotion—is therefore already presented as a "symbol of the Church." Likewise, the body assumed from the Virgin by the Word, as we confess from the perspective of the Cross and Resurrection, cannot be separated from the body which believers now are, having been born anew in the virgin Church. Given all the dimensions that we have seen going into this early theological reflection on Mary, we can perhaps now begin to understand the words of St John of Damascus: that "It is proper and true that we call the holy Mary the Theotokos ["God-bearer"], for this name expresses the entire mystery of the economy."[38]

NOTES

[1]Hermas *Vision* 1.2.1. Ed. and trans. K. Lake, LCL The Apostolic Fathers 2 (Cambridge, MA: Harvard University Press, 1976 [1913]).

[2]*Vision* 2.4.1.

[3]*Vision* 3.3.3.

[4]*Vision* 3.9.

[5]*Vision* 4.2.1.

[6]*Second Epistle of Clement* 14. Ed. and trans. K. Lake, LCL Apostolic Fathers 1 (Cambridge, MA: Harvard University Press, 1985 [1912]).

[7]The letter is preserved in Eusebius *Ecclesiastical History* 5.1–2. Ed. and trans. K. Lake, LCL (Cambridge, MA: Harvard University Press, 1980 [1926]).

[8]*Ecclesiastical History* 5.1.11.

[9]*Ecclesiastical History* 5.1.41.

[10]*Ecclesiastical History* 5.1.45–6.

[11]*Ecclesiastical History* 5.1.63.

[12]St Irenaeus of Lyons *Against the Heresies* 4.33.4.

[13]*Against the Heresies* 4.33.11.

[14]St Clement of Alexandria *Paedagogus* 1.6. Ed. O. Stählin, 3rd rev. ed. U. Treu, GCS 12 (Berlin: Akademie Verlag, 1972); Eng. trans. in ANF 2.

[15]Cf. A. McGowan, *Ascetic Eucharists: Food and Drink in Early Christian Ritual Meals* (Oxford: Oxford University Press, 1999), 107–115.

[16]St Clement of Alexandria *Stromata* 7.16, referring to the *Protoevangelium of James* 19.1–20.1, and citing *Pseudo-Ezekiel.*

[17]Tertullian *On the Soul* 43.10. Ed. J. H. Waszink (Amsterdam: North Holland Publishing Company, 1947); Eng. trans. in ANF 3.

[18]St Cyprian *On the Unity of the Church* 5–6. Ed. and trans. M. Bévenot, OECT (Oxford: Clarendon Press, 1971).

[19]Cf. Epiphanius *Panarion* 42.1.2–4. Trans. P. R. Amidon (New York and Oxford: Oxford University Press, 1990).

[20]Translation from *Η ΘΕΙΑ ΛΕΙΤΟΥΡΓΙΑ – The Divine Liturgy* (Oxford: Oxford University Press, 1995).

[21]Origen *Commentary on John* 1.23.

[22]St John Chrysostom *Homily 44 on Matthew* (on Mt 12.46–49). In NPNF first series, vol. 10.

[23]S. Brock, introduction to *Jacob of Serug: On the Mother of God,* trans. by M. Hansbury (Crestwood, NY: St Vladimir's Seminary Press, 1998), 9–10. Brock puts the emphasis slightly differently than I do: regarding the "dynamic view," he says that we can "regard Mary as reversing what Eve brought about, in which case Mary starts off, as it were, in the position into which Eve had reduced the human race, but though the Incarnation Mary is able to bring mankind back into Paradise, the pre-Fall state." That we can speak of Mary "achieving" this is surely only possible in the light of the redemption and re-creation that is the work of Christ alone. These two approaches to Mary are at the same time two different approaches to scripture. The dynamic view is grounded in a typological reading of scripture, one, that is, in which certain figures, events, or images are used to clarify others. The static view, on the other hand, as Brock puts it, tends "to take as literal truth what was originally intended to be the language of the symbol, poetry, metaphor, midrash." This is, as he characterizes it,

"a fundamentalist approach, and one that fossilizes typology, using it as a basis for creating fixed dogmas." On the other hand, "the typological approach to the Bible... is essentially a fluid one, refusing to be contained by dogmatic statements, on the one hand, or considerations of modern biblical scholarship and its findings on the other."

[24]St Ephrem of Syria *On the Resurrection*, as cited in L. Gambero, *Mary and the Fathers of the Church: The Blessed Virgin Mary in Patristic Thought*, trans. T. Buffer (San Francisco: Ignatius Press, 1999), 115.

[25]St Ephrem of Syria *Hymns on the Crucifixion* 4.17 (Gambero, *Mary*, 115).

[26]St Ephrem of Syria *Commentary on the Diatessaron* 12.5; trans. C. McCarthy (Oxford: Oxford University Press, 1993).

[27]St Ephrem of Syria *Hymns for the Unleavened Bread* 6.6–7 (Gambero, *Mary*, 115–16).

[28]St Ephrem of Syria *Hymns on the Nativity* 10.6–8. Trans. K. E. McVey (Mahwah, NJ: Paulist Press, 1989).

[29]See, for instance, the homilies delivered by St John Chrysostom in 386, discussed by T. Talley, *The Origins of the Christian Year*, 2nd rev. edn. (Collegeville, MN: Liturgical Press, 1991), 135–36.

[30]Evidenced on the statue of "Hippolytus"; cf. Talley, *Origins*, 9–10.

[31]Cf. Talley, *Origins*, 91–99, for variations on the "computation hypothesis."

[32]Augustine *On the Trinity* 4.2.9. Trans. E. Hill (Brooklyn, NY: New City Press, 1991).

[33]Cf. R. Brown, *The Birth of the Messiah: A Commentary on the Infancy Narratives in the Gospels of Matthew and Luke* (New York: Doubleday, 1993), and much more briefly, *An Adult Christ at Christmas: Essays on the Three Biblical Christmas Stories* (Collegeville, MN: Liturgical Press, 1978).

[34]Cf. T. Hopko, *Winter Pascha: Readings for the Christmas-Epiphany Season* (Crestwood, NY: St Vladimir's Seminary Press, 1984).

[35]St Hippolytus *On Christ and the Antichrist* 4. Ed. H. Achelis, GCS 1.2 (Leipzig: Hinrichs Verlag, 1987); Eng. trans. in ANF 5.

[36]*On Christ and the Antichrist* 61.

[37]St Maximus the Confessor *Commentary on the Lord's Prayer*. Ed. P. van Deun, CCSG 23 (Turnhout: Brepols, 1991), 50; Eng. trans. G. Berthold, CWS (London: SPCK, 1985).

[38]St John of Damascus *On the Orthodox Faith* 56 (= 3.12). Ed. B. Kotter, PTS 12 (Berlin and New York: De Gruyter, 1973); Eng. trans. F. H. Chase, FC 37 (Washington, DC: Catholic University of America Press, 1958).

CHAPTER FIVE

Glorify God in Your Body

So here we stand. We have taken many steps in our exploration of the mystery of Christ, and they have required much of us, challenging us to see many things, including ourselves, in a specific light: that of the crucified and exalted Christ, the Lord of all creation and its history. We have, however, only begun this exploration; were all the things that could be said to be written out, the world could not contain the books that would be written (cf. Jn 21.35). But, we at least now have an orientation and a framework, one that we have carefully established by looking closely at how it was that the disciples and apostles came to know that Jesus is Lord, and how those following in their footsteps continued this reflection.

Crucial to what we have seen is the recognition that theology is a confession, witnessing to the transforming power of God manifest in Christ: Light in darkness, Life in death, Word in flesh. What history would record as Jesus being put to death, theology confesses to be the very victory over death by one who gave himself for the life of the world. The basis for this confession is not a claim to "historical evidence" provided by the empty tomb or the resurrectional appearances: the empty tomb needs to be interpreted—in Matthew and Mark, the angel explained to the women that Jesus has risen, while Luke continues by describing how the disciples dismissed the women's report as an "idle tale" (Lk 24.11) and how the disciples failed to recognize the risen Jesus on the road to Emmaus (Lk 24.15–16), and John describes this same failure of recognition at the Sea of Tiberias (Jn 21.1–4). Theology begins, rather, with the opening of the scriptures by the risen Lord, so that his disciples can see how they all speak of him and the necessity of his Passion, and so be prepared to share in the meal to which he invites them, when he is recognized and disappears from sight (Lk 24.27–32), creating in them a desire for the Coming One. It is based on Peter's acknowledgment that he had betrayed Christ, that he was complicit in his death, but is nevertheless, and as a forgiven sinner, called to be an apostle, proclaiming the forgiveness of Christ, his mercy and his love—a new creation.

Such theology is a confession, acknowledging the work of God in Christ. But it is only possible if it is accompanied by a confession about oneself. As with the denier Peter, the persecutor Paul, and the prophet Isaiah before them, the reaction to the encounter with the Lord is the confession of one's own sinfulness—that we are, each, complicit in the death of Christ and his persecution and that he is our victim in each of our acts of violence and victimization. As we look to the scriptures, with the crucified and exalted Christ as our starting point, we can, only now, recognize that the world has lain in sin and death from the beginning, waiting to be saved and brought to true life by Christ. The truth of God revealed in Christ brings with it the revelation of the truth about human beings, both what they are called to be and that they have fallen from this high calling. The aim of theology always remains "the true understanding of things as they are, that is, of God and of the human being."[1]

But without undermining either the responsibility of humans for their apostasy (for it is, after all, only as the one that we have betrayed that Christ appears to us as Savior, our starting point) or the real catastrophe of death, this theological vision encompasses these all-too-human realities within the divine economy, known only retrospectively from the Cross, so that they can also be seen as divinely providential, as the necessary condition for the manifestation of the Lord and Savior Jesus Christ. "Salvation history," the narrative unfolded in scripture from the Creation and Fall onwards, is written from the perspective of the Cross.

The encounter with the Christ proclaimed "in accordance with the scriptures," in this manner, effects a similar transformation upon each person. If, as is sometimes said, the "self" of each person is their own past told from the perspective of the present, and that past acting in the present, then the encounter with Christ provides a new, and yet eternal, vantage point from which to narrate one's own past: we are invited to see our own past retold as our own "salvation history." In this, nothing is forgotten or left aside, as being somehow worthy only of being left behind, something that we would prefer to forget as too shameful or painful, but which even as "forgotten" continues to work negatively in our present. Rather, everything is encompassed within his economy: standing in the light of Christ, we can see him as having led us through our whole past, preparing us to encounter him. He alone knows the reason why he has led each of us on our particular path, for we still walk by faith, not by sight (2 Cor 5.7). But it is a faith that all things are in the hands of Christ, and that "in everything God works for good with those who love him" (Rom 8.28).

Within the limits of this world, it is death which seals the life-story of each person, revealing the final shape of that narrative and the identity of the person as they are remembered within this world. So also the life and identity of each person who turns to Christ is stamped or sealed by their baptism, in imitation of Christ's own death, dying to sin and this world. Yet for now their life and true identity "lies hidden with Christ in God" (Col 3.3), awaiting the decisive moment of their actual death, which will reveal whether their heart is still attached to this world, so making the transition of death painful, or whether it lies with God, so that they will be able to say, with Christ and the martyrs, "into thy hands I commend my spirit," a self-offering which makes their whole life and being, even in death, eucharistic. Until that moment, and in preparation for it, Christian life in this world is a continual practice of death, or rather, of life in death, taking up the Cross daily and laying down their life for others, considering themselves dead to this world but alive in Christ Jesus.

Practicing this life in death brings with it an increasing awareness of one's own sinfulness, and ultimately, even if only learned finally in the grave, a knowledge that our fallenness and brokenness extends to the very core of our being. Yet the knowledge of our own weakness, how it is that we are broken, is only made possible by the light of Christ, a light that simultaneously illumines the darkness, a strength made perfect in weakness. "It is," St Isaac of Syria affirmed, "a spiritual gift of God to be able to perceive one's own sins."[2] Moreover,

> the one who is conscious of his sins is greater than the one who profits the world by the sight of his countenance. The one who sighs over his soul for but one hour is greater than the one who raises the dead by his prayer while dwelling among human beings. The one who is deemed worthy to see himself is greater than the one who is deemed worthy to see the angels, for the latter has communion through his bodily eyes, but the former through the eyes of his soul.[3]

To plumb the depths of our fallenness is to scale the heights of divine love. Exploring the mystery of Christ in this way can only lead to the broken and contrite heart desired by God instead of sacrifices (Ps 51.16–17), but a heart which is now one of flesh, merciful and loving, rather than stone (Ezek 36.26).

Christians themselves, as forgiven sinners, are called to become wounded healers, extending the work of God to the whole world, to a point—the final, eschatological point—from which the whole of the world, and all the histories that are asserted in it, can be seen as encompassed within his economic providence. For some, such as those who have not encountered Christ during their lives in this world, or who have been presented with a false image of him, this may well occur after their deaths, and then they may well prove themselves to be more responsive to him than many who claim to be Christians now. When Christ finally comes again, "to judge the living and the dead," his judgment will be upon those who are "hardened in heart," unwilling to accept the salvation that he offers. Yet this judgment and offer of salvation is one that has already been definitively enacted: "Now is the judgment of the world, now shall the ruler of this world be cast out; and I, when I am lifted up from the earth, will draw all people to myself" (Jn 12.31–32). By the Cross, both now and in the eschaton, judgment is given, salvation offered, and the whole world drawn into unity.

So here we stand, "straining forward to what lies ahead" and pressing onwards in response to "the upward call of God in Christ Jesus" (Phil 3.14), being drawn out of ourselves by the coming Lord, all the while looking backwards to the Cross as the last publicly visible image of him in this world. In the light of his Passion as presented by the apostles and evangelists "in accordance with scripture," we can turn back to the treasury of the same scriptures—the Law, the Psalms, and the Prophets—to continue deepening our contemplation of the scriptural Christ, preparing ourselves to meet him in the meal to which he invites us, his broken body and spilt blood, and so become his body. The Church is "the garden [or paradise] planted in this world," according to St Irenaeus, in which we are given every tree, that is, every "scripture of the Lord," for our nourishment.[4] Just as the breath animated the human being at the beginning, so now the Spirit vivifies those in the Church, so that "where the Church is, there is the Spirit of God, and where the Spirit of God is, there is the Church and every kind of grace, and the Spirit is truth."[5] Guided by the Spirit promised by Christ, to bear witness to himself (Jn 15.26) and to lead the disciples into all truth by taking what is his and declaring it to them (Jn 16.13–14), we are able to read the scriptures and see in them—and, in their light, also in ourselves and in the whole world—the mystery of Christ.

The very fabric of the Church herself—what we see, hear, say, touch, and smell—provides a matrix, or womb, of such scriptural reflection, in the hymnography, iconography, and liturgical rites, fashioning us anew, as sons of God, born of the Virgin Mother. The apostolic tradition preserved by the Church—the continuity of the lived experience of the encounter with the scriptural Christ and the many expressions of this encounter—provides a further wealth of material for our nourishment. Surrounded by "a cloud of witnesses," we are encouraged to lay aside everything that holds us back and to run the race set before us with perseverance, "looking to Jesus the pioneer and perfecter of our faith, who for the joy that was set before him endured the cross, despising the shame, and is seated at the right hand of the throne of God" (Heb 12.1–1).

If the task, and power, of theology is to enable us to see things otherwise, in the light of Christ, the goal is the embodiment of this transformative power of God in the hearer, continuing the becoming-flesh of the Word, the continuing birth of Christ in this world. The mystery of Christ is an invitation to see him in the scriptures, then as the Lord of all creation and its history, and as our own Lord. Such theology elevates our minds to see all things anew, as the Creation of God, impregnated with and upheld by his Cross. If our own selves are to be rewritten in this way, standing in the mystery of Christ, then our task becomes to glorify God in our bodies.

THE AMBIVALENCE OF THE BODY

Much ink has been spilled decrying the negative attitude of Christianity towards the body, or, alternatively, responding to such charges by arguing that Christianity in fact has a positive view of the body. Both of these positions can certainly find much support in Christian literature. The ambivalence towards the body is shown most clearly in the ascetic literature. For instance, the desert hermit Abba Dorotheus is reported to have said about his body: "I kill it, lest it kills me";[6] yet, on the other hand, another desert dweller, Abba Poemen, said: "We have not been taught to kill our bodies, but to kill our passions."[7] Although there were undoubtedly a variety of positions regarding the body, it is not simply a matter of different figures taking different positions, for this apparent contradiction can be found within the same writer, even within the same sentence. The two affirmations are found together most emphatically in the *Ladder of Divine Ascent* by St John Climacus:

> By what rule or manner shall I bind this body of mine? . . . How can I hate him when my nature disposes me to love him? How can I break away from him when I am bound to him forever? How can I escape from him when he is going to rise with me? How can I make him incorrupt when he has received a corruptible nature? . . . He is my helper and my enemy, my assistant and my opponent, a protector and a traitor. . . . I embrace him. And I turn away from him. What is this mystery in me? What is the principle of this mixture of body and soul? How can I be my own friend and my own enemy?[8]

This ambivalence towards the body goes right back to the apostle Paul: the same Paul who cries out "who will deliver me from this body of death?" (Rom 7.24) and who sees the work of Christ as the destruction of "the body of sin" (Rom 6.6) also reminds us that "your body is a temple of the Holy Spirit' and so exhorts us to "glorify God in your body" (1 Cor 6.19–20), for Christ "will transfigure the body of our humiliation, so as to conform it to the body of his glory" (Phil 3.21). So, rather than simply marshalling evidence, to try to gauge which is the majority position, it is necessary, as we have seen so frequently in this book, to pay attention to *how* each statement is made and so see the fundamental ambiguity of the body, "this mystery in me," in St John's words.

This ambiguity is sometimes resolved by making a distinction between the "flesh" and the "body," not as different parts in the make-up of the human being, but as the totality of the human being viewed from two different perspectives: the word "body" being used for totality of the human being as made by and for God; the word "flesh" referring to the same totality, but viewed in its distance and opposition to God.[9] This is not strictly speaking correct. As we have already seen, the word "body" can be used both positively and negatively: the "body" which is a temple of the Spirit, and the "body" of sin and death. Likewise, the word "flesh," though often used in a negative sense, can also be used in a neutral sense, such as when Paul reports that he "did not confer with flesh and blood" (Gal 1.16), or even in both senses in the same statement: "Though we walk in the flesh, we do not war according to the flesh" (2 Cor 10.3).

However, while this ambiguity cannot be resolved into a contrast between "flesh" and "body," the observation does make two important points. First, that each of these words can be used to refer to the whole of the human being. As such, the word "flesh" does not simply refer to the "material" aspect of the human being, and likewise the "works of the flesh" does not solely, or even primarily, denote sinful bodily actions, but includes and, as we will see, even derives from, a mental or spiritual attitude, manifest in passions such as jealousy, anger, and selfishness (cf. Gal 5.16–21). It is "the mind of flesh" (or as in the RSV: "the mind that is set on the flesh") that is "hostile to God," and when Paul continues that "those who are in the flesh cannot please God" (Rom 8.7–8), he is speaking of those living with such a mind, rather than those who are embodied or enfleshed. The second point is that this ambivalence depends upon how our bodily and fleshly reality is viewed, and this, again, is a mental action.

St Athanasius, reflecting on the mystery of the Incarnation, describes well this ambiguity of the body. He discerns two reasons for the Word taking a body as his own, both of which we have extensively explored in this book: first, that by taking a body, the Word is able himself to undergo death, and so defeat death; second, that by doing this, the Word of God has made himself known.[10] A body was required for both of these actions, but it is his reason for the second that is of importance for us now:

> Once the mind of humans had descended to perceptible things, the Word submitted to being revealed through a body, that he might transfer humans to himself as a man, and turn their senses to himself, and that thenceforth, although they saw him as a man, he might

> persuade them through the works that he did that he was not only a man, but also God, and the Word and Wisdom of the true God.[11]

Because our minds had turned towards the things of sense-perception, the Word had to reveal himself in this manner, through a body, if human beings were going to be able to know the Word of God.

Extending this reflection to our original creation, St Athanasius observes that the human race was made "according to his own image through his own Word, our Savior Jesus Christ," fashioning "the human being to be perceptive and understanding of reality through his [i.e., the human being's] similarity to himself."[12] He then describes the "idyllic and truly blessed and immortal life" to which the human being had been called:

> For having no obstacle to the knowledge of the divine, he continuously contemplates by his purity the image of the Father, God the Word, after whose image he was made; he is awestruck when he grasps the providence which, through the Word, extends to the universe, being raised above the sensual and every bodily appearance, cleaving instead, by the power of his mind, to the divine and intelligible realities in heaven. For when the mind of human beings has no intercourse with bodies, nor has mingled with it, from outside, anything of their desires, but is entirely above them, as it was in the beginning, then, transcending the senses and all human things, it is raised up on high, and beholding the Word sees in him also the Father of the Word, taking pleasure in contemplating him and being renewed by its desire for him.[13]

Human beings were certainly created as embodied, that is, fleshly, beings, but in contrast to the irrational animals, human beings were also created with an ability to know God through his Word. Although such knowledge is only granted through transcending the senses (for the Word is not perceptible to the physical senses), there is no disparagement of the body itself: in this condition, human beings would not have lived by or for the body itself, and their minds would not have been driven by the sensual impressions and bodily desires that come from outside the mind. The ascetic thrust is not aimed at the body itself, but at the image of the body which is forced upon the mind from outside itself.

The reason for the present ambiguity of the body, and the reason (the starting point for this reflection, it must not be forgotten) why the Word revealed himself in and through the body, is that human beings chose not to remain in this state. As St Athanasius continues:

> In this way then, as has been said, did the Creator fashion the human race, and such did he wish it to remain. But men, contemptuous of the better things and shrinking from their apprehension, sought rather what was closer to themselves—and what was closer to them was the body and its sensations. So they turned their minds away from intelligible reality and began to consider themselves. And by considering themselves and holding to the body and the other senses, and deceived as it were in their own things, they fell into desire for themselves, preferring their own things to the contemplation of divine things. Spending their time in these things, and being unwilling to turn away from things close at hand, they imprisoned in bodily pleasures their souls which had become disordered and mixed up with all kinds of desires, while they wholly forgot the power they received from God in the beginning.[14]

God wished human beings to remain in the state that he had created them, but they chose otherwise, preferring what is closer to themselves, and this, St Athanasius specifies, is their body. Thus, far from denigrating the bodily reality of human existence, the body, for St Athanasius, is in fact "closer" to human beings: it is their "own" or what is "proper" to them.

If Athanasius does not speak of human beings transcending their minds or souls, it is not because these are somehow more divine, but rather that their mind or soul is the faculty whose orientation effects this transcendence: it is by our mind that we can come to know the Word of God and live appropriately to this knowledge. As human beings were to transcend themselves, not being concerned about "their own things," that is, the things of the body and this life, but rather occupying themselves with the Word of God, the body can even be said to be the locus of "the 'selfness' of being human."[15] However, human beings turned their attention towards themselves, to the body and its sense perception, receiving impressions from outside itself, and have consequently ended up being deceived even in "their own things." In this way, humans fell into the chaos of the fleshly desires of the body, forgetting what they had originally received from God. With their souls directed towards the body, in, by, and for itself, the body is now the very point of human separation from God, *not* because of its materiality, but because it has become an idol. It is as such, and *only as such*, that the body is to be treated as an "enemy," as St John Climacus counsels, or as Abba Dorotheus put it, "I kill my body, lest it kills me." They are not, therefore, speaking about the body itself, or anything which is proper to the body, but rather the way that the human mind sees the body, the image or idol it is fixated upon.

However, the same body which, seen one way, is an "enemy," an "opponent," and a "traitor," is also, seen another way, a "helper," an "assistant," and a "protector." The train of reasoning that led St Athanasius to conclude that the Word took a body because we had dispersed the power of our mind in the body and things of sense-perception, affirms, at the same time, that it is now in this very way that we have come to know the Word of God. The body is our means of knowing the Word of God, for he has revealed himself in and through a body. In doing so, the Word of God, the crucified and exalted Jesus Christ, has also demonstrated a way of being embodied, being human, towards which we must strive to become human ourselves. As such, the body is of prime importance in the spiritual struggle and is ultimately itself the "handiwork" fashioned by God in and through the struggle, and so, that in which God is glorified.

These two positive aspects of the body, as the arena in which the spiritual struggle is fought and as a new mode of bodily existence attained through such struggle, are both exemplified in the figure of St Antony the Great, whose *Life*, by St Athanasius, stands as a counterpart or mirror image of his work *On the Incarnation.* As the Word of God entered this world by taking a body as his own, in order to fight in the body and for the body, and so ensure victory over death and the devil for us who are in the body, so St Antony continues this battle, again in the body and for the body. Moreover, St Antony's own struggle is based upon the Incarnation and, in fact, is a continuation of that Incarnation. At the beginning of Antony's ascetic struggles, his asceticism is placed directly in the context of the victory won by Christ in the Incarnation:

> All these were things that took place to the enemy's shame. For he who considered himself to be like God was now made a buffoon by a mere youth, and he who vaunted himself against flesh and blood was turned back by a flesh-bearing man. Working with Antony was the Lord, who bore flesh for us, and gave to the body the victory over the devil, so that each of those who truly struggle can say, it is "not I, but the grace of God which is in me" [Gal. 2.20].[16]

Because of the Incarnation, the Lord has won the victory in and through and on behalf of the body, so that it is indeed the Lord himself who fights with us and ensures that the devil is defeated. The spiritual forces of the enemy, the powers that are not those of "flesh and blood" (cf. Eph 6.12), are nevertheless beaten by a "flesh-bearing man." Not only is the body involved in salvation, but it is the very means in which salvation is accomplished. This was St Antony's first victory against the devil—or rather, as the *Life* repeatedly corrects itself, the success of the Savior in the saint.

As St Antony continues his struggle with the devil, he goes out into the desert, not to escape the world and lose himself in contemplation, but to attack the devil on his own territory. After having spent twenty years barricaded in a deserted fortress, those who desired to emulate him broke down the door, and the saint emerged, in what is one of the most famous and forceful passages of the *Life*:

> Antony came forth as though from some shrine, having been led into divine mysteries and inspired by God. This was the first time he appeared from the fortress for those who came out to him. And when they beheld him, they were amazed to see that his body had maintained its former condition, neither fat from lack of exercise, nor emaciated from fasting and combat with demons, but was just as they had known him prior to his withdrawal. The state of his soul was one of purity, for it was not constricted by grief, nor relaxed by laughter or dejection. Moreover, when he saw the crowd, he was not annoyed any more than he was elated at being embraced by so many people. He maintained utter equilibrium, like one guided by the *logos* and steadfast in that which accords with nature.[17]

His years of severe asceticism and violent struggle with the devil have not resulted in the "mortification" of the body itself, nor in the attainment of a "supernatural" state. Rather, St Antony emerges from the fortress in an authentically "natural" state, neither fat nor emaciated. His soul is also in a state of purity, which is described not as being unable to feel pleasure or grief, but as not being swayed by such emotions. Having yielded himself so totally to God in this sacred shrine, he has within himself the one who has overcome "the world" and so is himself detached, interiorly and exteriorly, from the things of this world.

Given his natural state, it is not surprising that most translators have rendered the *logos* by which he is guided as "reason." But as the passage continues, it is clear that we should see here the Word of God, Christ himself, who is the subject of the verbs that follow:

> Through him the Lord healed many of those present who suffered from bodily ailments; others he purged of demons, and to Antony he gave grace in speech. Thus he consoled many who mourned, and others hostile to each other he reconciled in friendship, urging everyone to prefer nothing in the world above the love of Christ. And when he spoke and urged them to keep in mind the future goods and the affection in which we are held by God, "who did not spare his own Son, but gave him up for us all" [Rom. 8.32], he persuaded many to take up the solitary life. And so, from then on, there were monasteries in the mountains and the desert was made a city by monks, who left their own people and registered themselves for the citizenship in the heavens.

Emerging from the fortress, as from a tomb, St Antony has become totally delivered from worldly concerns and is now, in his body, the instrument of the Word, the one by whom Christ effects his work: healing the sick, consoling and reconciling others—almost an application of the messianic prophecies of Isaiah to St Antony, or rather, to Christ in him. Becoming an instrument of the Word—the Lord Jesus Christ—the saint attains the original goal of creation and so civilizes the desert with those who have their citizenship in heaven, uniting earth and heaven.

According to *The Life of St Antony*, this state of stable detachment distinguished Antony from all others, even in his physical appearance:

> It was not his physical dimensions that distinguished him from the rest, but the stability of character and the purity of soul. His soul being free of confusion, he held his outer senses also undisturbed, so that from the soul's joy his face was cheerful as well, and from the movements of the body it was possible to sense and perceive the stable condition of the soul.[18]

It is in and for the body that the victory was wrought by the Lord, and so it is in the body of the saint that we can see victory accomplished. The body, without any doubt, is involved in salvation and, more, is the very means of salvation. It, too, is to share, even now, in the life and body of the resurrected Lord. The description of St Antony as he approached death is just as emphatic and striking as the passage relating his emergence from the fortress:

> He never succumbed, due to old age, to extravagance in food, nor did he change his mode of dress because of frailty of the body, nor even bathe his feet with water, and yet in every way he remained free of injury. For he possessed eyes undimmed and sound, and he saw clearly. He lost none of his teeth—they simply had been worn to the gums because of the old man's great age. He also retained health in his feet and hands, and generally seemed brighter and of more energetic strength than those who make use of baths and a variety of foods and clothing.[19]

The vitality of Antony as he approached death is a clear sign of the anticipation or foretaste of the resurrectional incorruptibility granted in Christ already now, in his body. This, together with all the virtues of the saint, as described in the *Life*, such as healing others and exorcising demons, are all gifts, granted in the wake of the victory won by Christ himself, and, as such, express the anticipation of the salvation already available in Christ, in the body.

The same points as those we have seen in the case of St Antony, the founder of monasticism in the fourth century, are made in later spirituality, especially hesychasm, the quest for the stillness or silence in which one encounters God: "Be still and know that I am God" (Ps 46.10). Playing upon the Greek image of a soul trapped in a body, St John Climacus refers to the body as the cell of the hesychast and, in so doing, turns the value of the image upside down. According to St John, "The cell of the hesychast is the body that surrounds him, and within him is the dwelling place of knowledge."[20] The body is the cell to which one must return to engage in prayer, for it is the locus of knowledge. As such, St John gives the following definition of what he considers to be the true hesychast:

> A hesychast is one who strives to confine what is incorporeal within the body, paradoxical as this is.[21]

For St. John, to keep all the powers of the soul—thought, imagination, desire, and so on—enclosed within the confines of oneself, one's own body is the very definition of a hesychast. Such a one will, like St Antony, always be calm and collected wherever they are, able to abide in love without being swayed by the impressions of the world and the passions that they generate: "He, who in actually going out does not go out, is gentle and wholly in a house of love."[22]

This perspective was picked up by St Gregory Palamas in the fourteenth century, in the context of defending the methods of hesychastic prayer and, in particular, the utility of particular bodily practices in such prayer. After quoting the definition of a hesychast given by St John, St Gregory comments:

> And our spiritual fathers have rightly taught us things in harmony with this. For if the hesychast does not enclose his intellect within his body, how can he possess within himself the One who is invested with the body and who as its natural form penetrates all structurally organized matter? The determined exterior aspect of this matter—the material body—cannot enshrine the essence of the intellect until the material body itself truly lives by adopting a form of life appropriate to the union with the intellect.[23]

The importance of the body is, again, correlated to the Incarnation: it is because the Word himself has taken a body, dwelling in it and expressing himself through it, that we are to focus our lives in our body, with the corollary that this also demands the appropriate behavior in and for the body. St Gregory does not make clear what he means by saying that the One who has taken a body, the Word, "as its natural form penetrates all structurally organized manner." But given what we have seen in earlier chapters regarding the form of the cross perceived in all creation—the height, depth, breadth, and length of the cross being the four basic coordinates of all "structurally organized matter"—it would seem to refer to the Cross, emphasizing the point that it is only as the crucified and exalted one that we know the Word of God to have taken a body, and that the life now demanded of us in the body, appropriate to its union with the mind, is that of taking up the Cross.

In his particular context, St Gregory's concern was to defend the crouched bodily posture adopted by the hesychasts in prayer: sitting on a low stool, with the chin resting on the chest. This would have seemed a rather strange position for prayer, for standing had always been considered the appropriate posture for prayer; it earned them the nickname "navel-gazers." But in his justification of this position, St Gregory makes a more general, and important, point. Apart from appealing to Elijah on Mount Carmel for a biblical precedent (cf. 1 Kgs 18.42), St Gregory makes the comment that "a great teacher has said that after the transgression, our inner being naturally adapts itself to outward forms."[24] By adopting a circular posture, the mind is directed back upon itself, to become aware of its own inner world in a circular movement. That is, our outward posture has an effect upon the inward activity of our mind; the two are neither independent nor unrelated. There is an undeniable correspondence between the inner and the outer aspects of the human being, evident in such common phenomena as the increased rate of breathing when excited, or altering one's inner state by controlling the outward aspects such as our physical posture and processes such as breathing. The very form of the body is involved in the act of prayer, in many practices that we do without thinking, such as bowing or prostrating to express, and increase, contrition or raising the hands in thanksgiving. While St Athanasius emphasized, in the figure of St Antony, that his inward state manifested itself in his outward bearing, so the Byzantine hesychastic writers drew attention to the reverse side of this relation, that our body itself has a contribution to make to our spiritual life.[25]

Finally, the later Byzantine writers also reaffirmed the other point regarding the body that we saw in the case of St Antony, that the body is called to participate even now in the life of the resurrection, albeit in an anticipatory manner, still awaiting the time of its fulfillment in the resurrection. As the apostles saw the light of the Transfiguration, which is interpreted as the light of the kingdom to come, with their bodily eyes, so also our body is to participate even now in the eschatological blessings. So, St Gregory wrote, in the *Hagioretic Tome*, signed by the monks of Athos as a statement of their theology, that

> if, in the age to come, the body is to share with the soul in the ineffable blessings, then it is evident that in this world as well it will also share according to its capacity in the grace mystically and ineffably bestowed by God upon the purified intellect, and it will experience the divine in conformity with its nature. For once the soul's passible [i.e., changeable, potentially sinful] aspect is transformed and sanctified—but not reduced to a deathlike condition—through it the dispositions and activities of the body are also sanctified, since body and soul share a conjoint existence.[26]

The vision of God, and the transfiguration in that vision, is to be shared by both soul and body. But this depends on the "passible aspect" of the soul being transformed and sanctified, so enabling the body to be used properly.

THE AMBIVALENCE OF THE PASSIONS

Having considered the ambivalence of the body—how the body becomes an idol, yet is also the locus of the revelation of God, and thus the place in which we are to glorify God—we can now turn to the words of Abba Poemen, that "we have not been taught to kill our bodies, but to kill our passions." What then are the passions that are to be put to death, and is there an ambivalence here parallel to that of the body?

As with the body, the Fathers speak of the "passions" in terms which can often seem contradictory. It is sometimes said that some Fathers followed the Stoics, for whom the passions are essentially disordered movements of the body contrary to nature, inherently unnatural, needing to be totally eradicated, while others adopted an Aristotelian position, which held that the passions are something neutral in themselves, capable of being used either for good or for evil, needing only to be educated. Such a contrast is in some ways misleading, not paying sufficient attention to the way in which different writers employ the term "passion," and so directing attention away from the real source of ambivalence.

Some writers do indeed use the term "passion" to refer to the basic drives, movements, and affections of the human being, such as the capacity for erotic love or anger. Such faculties are certainly held to be neutral in themselves; the issue is the way in which they are employed. When other writers speak of having to eradicate the "passions," however, they are not speaking of the same thing. Rather they use this term, "passion," to refer to such drives and affections when they are no longer moving in accord with reason or the Word (*logos* in both cases). What the former writers speak of as "passions," these others refer to by various other words, such as "impulse" or "appetite." Clement of Alexandria makes this point clear:

> Those skilled in such matters distinguish impulse from desire and assign the latter, as being irrational, to pleasure and licentiousness; and impulse, as being a rational movement, they assign to the necessities of nature.[27]

"Impulse" is a "rational (*logikos*) movement," one that accords with nature, while "desire" is no longer "rational" but "irrational" (*alogos*) and hedonistic, deriving from pleasure and licentiousness. Clement makes a similar distinction elsewhere:

> Appetite is the movement of the mind to or from something. Passion is an excessive appetite, exceeding the measures of the Word, or appetite unbridled and disobedient to reason. Passions then are a movement of the soul contrary to nature in disobedience to the Word.[28]

So, for Clement, while the "passions" have their origins in the natural functions and urges, it is their excessive use *contrary* to reason or to the Word, and brought about by pleasure and disobedience, that characterize the passions. This is an important point, for it means that in both ways of speaking, it is not the movements, the urges, the functions, nor appetites of nature that are at issue in the ascetic struggle, but rather the way that they are employed.

In distinguishing between the "impulses" or "appetites," on the one hand, and the "passions," on the other hand, Clement of Alexandria was developing an analysis begun already by the Stoics.[29] The important point that he, and later Fathers, pick up from this analysis is that the "passions" are not simply blind movements of the body or stirrings of affection. Rather, the "passions" have an important cognitive component: they derive from and embody a form of false judgment or false belief—they are the movements of the body no longer in accord with reason (*logos*). Of course, in appropriating this analysis for Christianity, the notion of the *logos*, according to which what is "natural" is determined, receives a very specific content—the Word of God. Being able to discern the "passions," and so "kill" them on behalf of the body and for the body, is primarily a battle fought with our own perceptions of the body and its movements, countering the false beliefs and perceptions that give rise to the passions. Since the "*Logos*" by which this is determined is the Word of God, Jesus Christ, it is necessary to ground this ascetic struggle in "the true understanding of things as they are, that is, of God and of the human beings," to use St Irenaeus' words once again.[30]

If one does not recognize that the struggle is ultimately with one's own perceptions, then one is left waging war on one's own nature. In such a battle, one can attempt to draw a distinction, as some have done, between, on the one hand, a "natural asceticism," which attempts to reduce the material needs of life to its natural minimum, living in total simplicity, without deliberately causing the body to suffer, and, on the other hand, an "unnatural asceticism," which takes special effort to cause suffering to the body, mortifying it by contrived practices, such as that of Abba Joseph of Panephysis who mixed sea water with the river water that he drank.[31] The point of this contrast is well taken, though it is somewhat misdirected. In the anecdote which relates the practice of Abba Joseph, the point of describing his practice was to teach a lesson to Eulogius: although Eulogius was regarded by his disciples as a great ascetic, eating only bread and salt, he was instructed by Abba Joseph "in discernment of thoughts and in controlling all the merely human in himself; so he became more balanced and ate whatever was brought to him and learnt how to work in secret." The struggle is, once again, with our thoughts. Distinguishing between "natural" and "unnatural" asceticism, on the other hand, regards the problem, in both cases, as located in the body itself, and its appetites and functions, which need to be limited and constrained, rather than in the mind which distorts these appetites and functions for its own purposes. It is not enough to speak of educating rather than eradicating the "passions," if by "passions" one is thinking of the urges, movements, or appetites proper to the body, rather than these movements as they are employed by the mind in perverse and unnatural ways.

As the apostle Paul put it with regard to the food offered to idols: "Food will not commend us to God. We are no worse off if we do not eat, and no better off if we do. Only take care lest this liberty of yours somehow become a stumbling block to the weak" (1 Cor. 8.8–9). Whether one eats meat or vegetables, drinks water or wine, does not matter; the attitude one has towards one's food and drink determines whether one is a glutton or not, a drunkard or not, and the overriding concern is the effect that one's own practice has on others, for everything should be done in love for the building up of the body (cf. 1 Cor 12–13). Likewise, when the Fathers talk about disciplining the body through asceticism, they are not so much referring to the actual, physical body with its natural and proper urges and movements, but rather this body as it is seen by a fleshly mind, a mind which is passionately attached to this body and its functions, a mind which seeks its pleasures in and through the body. The overarching determinant for any behavior, as with the lesson taught by Abba Joseph's asceticism, is the edification of others and the building up of the body of Christ.

St Gregory of Nyssa, in his work *On the Making of the Human Being*, provides a full discussion of how the "passions" have their ground in the body and its impulses and appetites, but come into existence only by the misuse of these natural faculties by the mind. He begins by apparently connecting the passions straightforwardly with our bodily nature:

> Our love of pleasure took its beginning from our being made like to the irrational creation and was increased by the transgressions of human beings, becoming the parent of so many varieties of sins arising from pleasure as we cannot find among the irrational animals.[32]

That is, although human beings have a bodily existence akin to that of the irrational animals, only in our case has this led to the passions and sin. The sinfulness of the passions, therefore, does not reside in the materiality of the body, that which is created by God, but in the manner in which the mind regards and abuses the body and its impulses and appetites. He continues by discussing a few examples:

> Thus the rising of anger in us is indeed akin to the impulse of the brutes, but it grows by the alliance of thought; for thence come malignity, envy, deceit, conspiracy, hypocrisy; all these are the result of the evil husbandry of the mind; for if the passion were divested of the aid it receives from thought, the anger that is left behind is short-lived and not sustained, like a bubble, perishing straightway as soon as it comes into being. Thus the greediness of swine introduces covetousness, and the high spirit of the horse becomes the origin of pride; and all the particular forms that proceed from the want of reason in brute nature become vice by the evil use of the mind.

The impulses of the nature which we share with the irrational animals become sinful passions by the evil use of our mind, that which distinguishes us from the irrational animals, in whom such things are consequently never manifested. This is the cognitive element in the passions that we considered earlier. Together with specifying where the problem lies, St Gregory suggests that if this mistaken element of thought is corrected, the passion would disappear, like a burst bubble.

St Gregory continues to develop this thought, by examining what might then come about:

> So, likewise, on the contrary, if reason, instead, assumes sway over such emotions, each of them is transmuted to a form of virtue; for anger produces courage, terror caution, fear obedience, hatred aversion from vice, the power of love the desire for what is truly beautiful; high spirit in our character raises our thought above the passions, and keeps it from bondage to what is base; yea, the great Apostle, even, praises such a form of mental elevation when he bids us constantly to "think those things which are above" [Col 3.2]; and so we find that every such motion, when elevated by loftiness of mind, is conformed to the beauty of the divine image.[33]

Every movement, appetite, or impulse of our human nature unequivocally has its God-given purpose, and every such movement, when it is directed by a mind set on high, manifests a divine beauty.

St John Climacus, in his *Ladder of Divine Ascent*, makes exactly the same point:

> God neither caused nor created evil and, therefore, those who assert that certain passions come naturally to the soul are quite wrong. What they fail to realize is that we have taken natural attributes of our own and turned them into passions. For instance, the seed which we have for the sake of procreating children is abused by us for the sake of fornication. Nature has provided us with anger as something to be turned against the serpent, but we have used it against our neighbor. We have a natural urge to excel in virtue, but instead we compete in evil. Nature stirs within us the desire for glory, but that glory is of a heavenly kind. It is natural for us to be arrogant—against the demons. Joy is ours by nature, but it should be joy on account of the Lord and for the sake of doing good to our neighbor. Nature has given us resentment, but that ought to be against the enemies of our souls. We have a natural desire for food, but surely not for profligacy.[34]

Eating itself is natural to a human being, and there is nothing wrong with enjoying the food one eats; it is gluttony, rather, which is a passion and a vice. As St John Climacus describes it, gluttony is a false opinion about the way things are: "Gluttony is hypocrisy of the stomach. Filled, it moans about scarcity; stuffed and crammed, it wails about its hunger. Gluttony thinks up seasonings, creates sweet recipes. . . . Gluttony has a deceptive appearance: it eats moderately but wants to gobble everything at the same time."[35] Gluttony has its own cognitive element, and one which is based in deception. Through the practice of fasting, controlling the stomach, one does not simply reduce one's dietary intake to the minimum possible, but instead learns to break through the hypocrisy of the stomach, to know that one will not die if one does not eat as one has become accustomed to do. The "hypocrisy" of the stomach is not located in the bodily organ itself, but in the mind's relation to the stomach.

St Gregory's statement, that "every motion, when elevated by loftiness of mind, is conformed to the beauty of the divine image," is an important one, affirming without qualification the possibility of the transfiguration of the whole of our God-created being. We have already seen St John Climacus affirm that the "seed," though most often employed for the sake of fornication, was given to human beings for the sake of procreation. Elsewhere St John hints about a possible use of this faculty beyond that of procreation:

> I have watched impure souls mad for physical love but turning what they know of such love into a reason for repentance and transferring that same capacity for love to the Lord. I have watched them master fear so as to drive themselves unsparingly towards the love of God. That is why, when talking of that chaste harlot, the Lord does not say, "because she feared," but rather, "because she loved much" she was able to drive out love with love" [Lk 7.47].[36]

Love itself, the same capacity which manifests itself in impassioned physical love, should be directed towards the Lord: "Lucky is the one who loves and longs for God as a smitten lover does for his beloved."[37] Stated more generally, "Physical love (*eros*) can be a paradigm of the longing for God."[38]

If such is the meaning of the word "passion," then the goal towards which asceticism strives, dispassion (*apatheia*), is not the eradication of the natural movements, impulses, or appetites proper to human nature, but the eradication of the sinful abuse of these faculties, the "passions," in a reaffirmation of their proper, God-given, use. As such, to be dispassionate is not, as some have thought (or been accused of thinking), to have attained a completely inert state, as dead as a stone, but to have arrived at a freedom from passion, from being moved passively, a freedom in which we can once again be fully active, acting as is proper to human beings: *apatheia* "connotes not repression but reorientation, not inhibition but freedom; having overcome the passions, we are free to be our true selves, free to love others, free to love God."[39]

Two final points about this state of dispassion should be noted. First, its eschatological color: it is a state which already anticipates the resurrection, as did St Antony when he emerged from his fortress. St John Climacus even defines *apatheia* in such terms, as "the resurrection of the soul prior to that of the body."[40] Second, *apatheia* is intimately connected with love, for it provides the freedom within which one can once again act in the manner proper to a human being, exemplified primarily and paradigmatically by Jesus Christ, that is, living on behalf of others and giving his very life and being for them. In fact, in the words of St John Climacus once again, "Love, *apatheia*, and adoption are distinguished by name, and name alone."[41]

"GOD CREATES, HUMAN BEINGS ARE CREATED"

Having established a proper perspective and orientation for viewing our body and its movements, we can now see why it is that the apostle directs us to "glorify God in your body" (1 Cor 6.20). Christian theology begins and ends with the mystery of Christ, the crucified and exalted Lord as preached by the apostles "in accordance with scripture." The revelation of God occurs in and through what Jesus Christ has done as human, and a theology which keeps focused on this Word of God enables the transformative power of God revealed in Christ to be at work in us as well, fashioning us, in the body, to the full stature of a true human being. The whole economy of God, embracing both creation *and* salvation—including sin, apostasy, and death—works to fashion us into the image and likeness of God, Jesus Christ himself, extending his bodily presence in the world, the incarnation of the Word or the birth of Christ in us.

"The work of God is the fashioning of the human being," St Irenaeus affirms[42]—this work is announced in Genesis, completed on the Cross, and continued in ourselves as we take up the Cross. The eternal glory of God, which Christ had with the Father before all creation, is revealed in this world in the Passion, the crucifixion and exaltation of Christ, and this is, at the same time, the first manifestation of a true human being within creation: "Behold the man" (Jn 19.5). In this way, St Irenaeus can affirm that "the living human being is the glory of God" and, further, that "the life of humans is to see God,"[43] that is, to be elevated in mind by a true theology; to be able to behold, if not fully comprehend, the glory of God; and so be conformed to his image in our own body.

How then, inscribed within this economy, are we to become truly human—to become a god? The answer is contained in the same structure: "God creates, human beings are created."[44] Those who refuse to accept that they are what God has created them to be—"humans capable of passions"—wanting instead to be as they imagine God to be, betray, on the one hand, an ignorance of the divine economy, in which Christ has shown what it is to be God and to be truly human, and, on the other hand, a lack of confidence in their Creator.[45] They establish their own agenda for becoming what they want to be. To become truly human—to become a god—we must allow God to fashion us, and this requires that we be open and responsive to the work of God. One last word from St Irenaeus, whose theology has informed so much of this work, puts it well:

> How then will you be a god, when you are not yet made human? How perfect, when only recently begun? How immortal, when in mortal nature you did not obey the Creator? It is necessary for you first to hold the rank of human, and then to participate in the glory of God. For you do not create God, but God creates you. If, then, you are the work of God, await the Hand of God, who does everything at the appropriate time—the appropriate time for you, who are being

> made. Offer to him your heart, soft and pliable, and retain the shape with which the Fashioner shaped you, having in yourself his Water, lest you turn dry and lose the imprint of his fingers. By guarding this conformation, you will ascend to perfection; the mud in you will be concealed by the art of God. His Hand created your substance; it will gild you, inside and out, with pure gold and silver, and so adorn you that the King himself will desire your beauty. But if, becoming hardened, you reject his art and being ungrateful towards him, because he made you human, ungrateful, that is, towards God, you have lost at once both his art and life. For to create is the characteristic of the goodness of God; to be created is characteristic of the nature of human beings. If, therefore, you offer to him what is yours, that is, faith in him and subjection, you will receive his art and become a perfect work of God. But if you do not believe in him, and flee from his Hands, the cause of imperfection will be in you who did not obey, and not in him who called you. For he sent messengers to call people to the feast; but those who did not obey deprived themselves of his royal banquet [cf. Mt 22.3].[46]

Rather than hardening ourselves, trying to become what we want to be, we must remain pliable, open, and responsive to the creative activity of God: we must learn "to relax in the hands of God, to let God be the creator."[47] Such also was the wisdom of the desert fathers. When Abba Agathon was approached by someone suffering from the temptation of fornication, his advice was: "Go, cast your weakness before God and you shall find rest."[48] Abba Poemen likewise stated that "to throw yourself before God, not to measure your progress, to leave behind all self-will: these are the instruments for the work of the soul."[49] The rest granted in this manner again has an eschatological coloring tone; it is anticipated in this life, entered into in death, and flowers in the age to come. Such rest is only granted by an act of trust, a trusting obedience, the "faith and subjection" which St Irenaeus specifies is that which we can and must offer. Such faith is not merely blind obedience nor a resigned helplessness, for it knows that all things, as we have seen, are in the hands of God "who works everything for good in those who love him" (Rom 8.28). Such is the invitation offered to us by the mystery of Christ, who calls out to us: "Come unto me all who labor and are heavy laden, and I will give you rest" (Mt 11.28).

NOTES

[1]St Irenaeus of Lyons *Against the Heresies* 5.2.3. Ed. and French trans. A. Rousseau et al, SC 263–4, 293–4, 210–11, 100, 152–3 (Books 1–5 respectively) (Paris: Cerf, 1979, 1982, 1974, 1965, 1969). Eng. trans. in ANF 1.

[2]St Isaac of Syria *Ascetical Homilies* 74. (Boston: Holy Transfiguration Monastery, 1984).

[3]*Ascetical Homilies* 64.

[4]St Irenaeus *Against the Heresies* 5.20.2.

[5]*Against the Heresies* 3.24.1.

[6]Palladius *Lausiac History* 2.2. Trans. R. T. Meyer, ACW 34 (Westminster, MD: Newman Press, 1965).

[7]*Sayings of the Desert Fathers* Poemen 184. Trans. B. Ward, rev. edn. CS 59 (Kalamazoo, MI: Cistercian Publications, 1987).

[8]St John Climacus *The Ladder of Divine Ascent* step 15. Classics of Western Spirituality (Ramsey, NJ: Paulist Press, 1982).

[9]Classically stated by J. A. T. Robinson, *The Body: A Study in Pauline Theology* (London: SCM Press, 1952), cf. 31.

[10]These two rationales are explored by St Athanasius in *On the Incarnation* 3–10 and 11–19 respectively. Ed. and trans. R.W. Thomson, OECT (Oxford: Clarendon Press, 1971).

[11]*On the Incarnation* 16.

[12]St Athanasius *Against the Pagans* 3. Ed. and trans. R.W. Thomson, OECT (Oxford: Clarendon Press, 1971).

[13]Ibid.

[14]Ibid.

[15]K. Anatolios, *Athanasius: The Coherence of His Thought* (New York: Routledge, 1998), 64.

[16]St Athanasius *The Life of St Antony* 5. Ed. and French trans. G. J. M. Bartelink, SC 400 (Paris: Cerf, 1994); Eng. trans. R. C. Gregg, CWS (New York: Paulist Press, 1980).

[17]*Life of St Antony* 14.

[18]*Life of St Antony* 67.

[19]*Life of St Antony* 93.

[20]St John Climacus *The Ladder of Divine Ascent* step 27.

[21]Ibid.

[22]Ibid.

[23]St Gregory Palamas *Triads* 1.2.6. Ed. P. K. Christou, vol. 1, 2nd ed. (Thessalonika, 1988); Eng. trans. N. Gendle, CWS (Mahwah, NJ: Paulist Press, 1983).

[24]*Triads* 1.2.8; Elijah is mentioned in *Triads* 1.2.10.

[25]For further discussion see Kallistos Ware, "Praying with the Body: The Hesychast Method and Non-Christian Parallels," *Sobornost* 14.2 (1992): 6–35.

[26]*The Hagioretic Tome* 6. Ed. P. K. Christou, vol. 2 (Thessalonika, 1988); Eng. trans. in *The Philokalia*, vol 4, trans. G. E. H. Palmer, P. Sherrard, K. Ware (London: Faber and Faber, 1995), 418–25.

[27]Clement of Alexandria *Stromata* 4.18(4.18.117.5). Stromata VII–VIII, Ed. O. Stählin, 2nd ed. rev. L.Früchtel and U.Treu,GCS 17 (Berlin: Akademie Verlag, 1970). Trans. in ANF 2.

[28]*Stromata* 2.13 (2.13.59.6).

[29]Cf. M. Nussbaum, *The Therapy of Desire* (Princeton: Princeton University Press, 1994), chap. 10.

[30]St Irenaeus *Against the Heresies* 5.2.3.

[31]*Sayings of the Desert Fathers* Eulogius the Priest.

[32]St Gregory of Nyssa *On the Making of Man* 18.4. PG 44.193; Eng. trans. in NPNF series 2, vol. 5.

[33]*On the Making of Man* 18.5.

[34]St John Climacus *The Ladder of Divine Ascent* step 26.

[35]*Ladder* step 14.

[36]*Ladder* step 5.

[37]*Ladder* step 30.

[38]*Ladder* step 26.

[39]Bishop Kallistos (Ware), Introduction to *St John Climacus: The Ladder of Divine Ascent*, 32.

[40]St John Climacus *Ladder of Divine Ascent* step 29.

[41]*Ladder* step 30.

[42]St Irenaeus *Against the Heresies* 5.15.2.

[43]*Against the Heresies* 4.20.7.

[44]*Against the Heresies* 4.11.2.

[45]*Against the Heresies* 4.38.4.

[46]*Against the Heresies* 4.39.2–3.

[47]D. Minns, *Irenaeus* (London: Geoffrey Chapman, 1994), 64.

[48]*Sayings of the Desert Fathers* Agathon 21.

[49]*Sayings of the Desert Fathers* Poemen 36.

POSTSCRIPT

A Premodern Faith for a Postmodern Era

Having explored the mystery of Christ, not indeed comprehensively, but hopefully with a certain rigor, beginning with the way in which the evangelists present the disciples as coming to know Christ, it seems appropriate to offer a postscript epitomizing the paradigm shift undertaken here, indicating how such theology differs from the approach which characterizes much modern theology.

As I suggested in the Preface, a lot of modern theology, despite all its variety, operates in a manner that can only be described as an odd mixture of metaphysics and mythology. Forgetting the basic principle that conclusions without the arguments that lead to them are at best ambiguous, such theology begins with the doctrine of God as Trinity, and then, abandoning the supposedly "primitive" exegetical methods of premodern theology, in and through which the doctrine of the Trinity was elaborated, retells the interaction between God and the world in a modern historical manner. Having posited the existence of the Trinity, the next step is to describe creation, the paradisiacal life of Adam and Eve, the tragedy of the Fall, the long history of salvation in which God, usually in the person of the "pre-incarnate Logos," appeared to Abraham, and spoke with Moses and through the Prophets, culminating in the incarnation of one of the Trinity, who returned to the Father after the Passion, sending the Spirit to guide the Church through the remaining time of human history, until the second coming. Such an approach can, given the limitations of any pictorial representation, be represented by the sketch in figure 1 on page 175.

The move to such an approach to theology seems to begin with St Augustine, who, having inherited the results of the fourth-century debates rather than living through them, is the first to claim that the theophanies of the Old Testament could be manifestations of any of the three persons of the Trinity, or the Trinity itself, the one Lord God, or, instead, a created mediator.[1] By the Middle Ages, Peter Lombard, following the logic of this approach, asserted that the Father or the Spirit equally could have become incarnate; as Karl Rahner pointed out, it is difficult to say why it was the Son who became incarnate.[2] The "Incarnation" is the becoming-human of a divine person which could have been otherwise, a way in which God chose to reveal himself at a particular moment, for a particular, separate or discrete, work.

In short, such an approach to theology undermines the very gospel itself. The witness of the apostles and the Fathers of the fourth century following them—the supposed architects of our "Trinitarian theology" (I put this phrase in quotation marks, because none of them thought of themselves as elaborating a "Trinitarian theology")—is simply that *what* we see in Christ, as proclaimed by the apostles, is *what* it is to be God, yet *other* than the God whom Christ calls upon as Father and makes known through, and is himself made known by, the Holy Spirit. It could not have been otherwise, nor could it now be, for this is how the God of the Christian faith *is*.

In the modern paradigm, the second person of the Trinity turns out to be a temporal being, who did various things as the "pre-incarnate Logos" before becoming incarnate as Jesus Christ; his existence as Jesus Christ is but an episode in a longer biography. Ironically, this is the very position that the Council of Nicaea and those following it were at pains to refute![3] Moreover, where we stand in such a picture is left unspecified: what privileged vantage point do we have to describe the being of God prior to creation and then to speak of the "history" of his interaction with creation? The result really is, as I have suggested, an odd mixture of metaphysics and mythology.

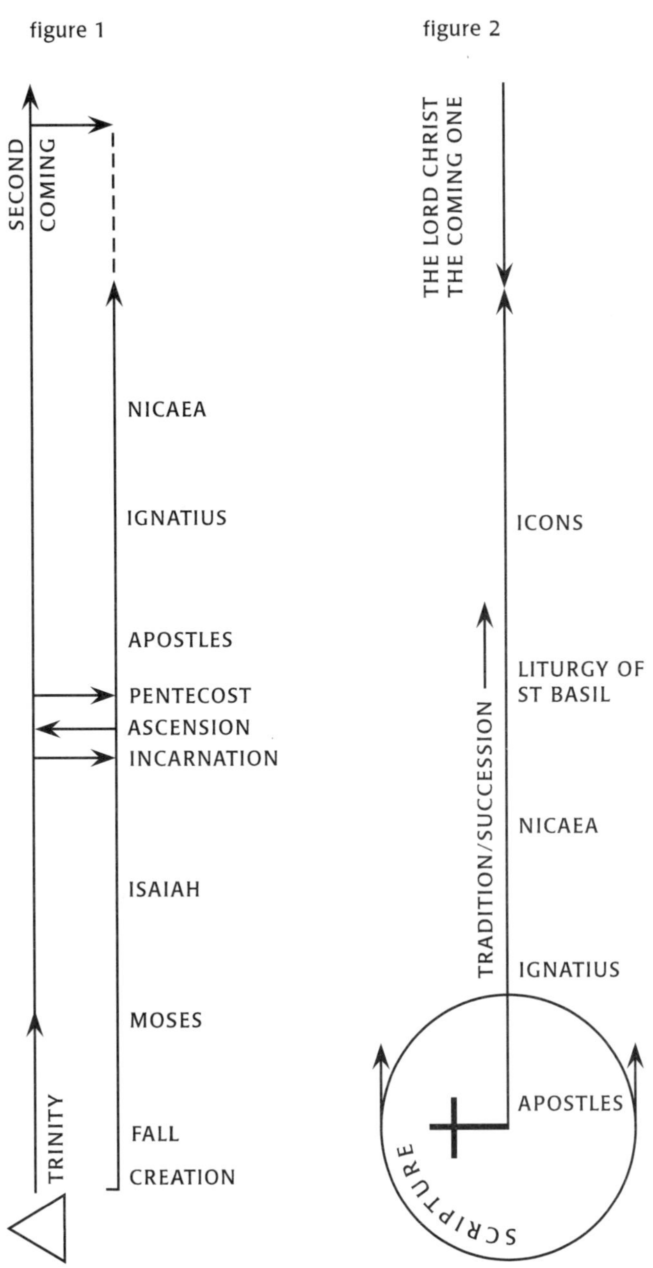
figure 1
SECOND
COMING
NICAEA
IGNATIUS
APOSTLES
PENTECOST
ASCENSION
INCARNATION
ISAIAH
MOSES
TRINITY
FALL
CREATION
figure 2
THE LORD CHRIST
THE COMING ONE
ICONS
LITURGY OF
ST BASIL
TRADITION/SUCCESSION
NICAEA
IGNATIUS
APOSTLES
SCRIPTURE

A further modification resulting from putting a "premodern" theology in "modern" clothing is that it obscures the person of Christ and his Cross. It became almost the consensus position of theology at the end of the last century that to be in the image of God is to be a person in communion, imaging the three persons in communion in heaven: Christ has been put out of the picture, except insofar as he is one of the persons in communion in heaven. But, the New Testament, and the Fathers following the apostles, are emphatic that Christ alone *is* the image of God, and that to be *in* the image of God is to be conformed to his image, by being crucified with him, taking up the Cross.

If, however, we follow the way in which the apostles proclaimed the gospel, and the manner in which the Fathers thought through this—following the way in which they did theology, rather than simply appropriating for our own purposes the formulas they produced as a result—we have a very different picture. However the disciples had been reading scripture prior to the moment in which the crucified and exalted Lord opened the scriptures—to show how they all spoke about him and the necessity of his Passion—they had not seen or expected this. Likewise, whatever the disciples knew about Jesus Christ prior to his Passion, they still had not come to understand him as the Lord. Similarly, whatever human beings might have known of God from creation, prior to the Passion, they did not recognize him, preferring instead to idolize creation rather than worship the Creator. The way that scripture was read and creation regarded, prior to the Passion, serves, as we have seen, to "consign us to sin," so that we might be ready to receive Christ as our Savior.

Neither the Crucifixion, nor the empty tomb, nor even the appearances of the risen Christ are in themselves the starting point for Christian faith: the leader of the apostles denied Christ; the myrrh-bearing women did not understand the significance of the empty tomb; and the disciples on the road to Emmaus did not recognize the risen Lord. Rather, only when the disciples finally understood the Passion "in accordance with scripture" are they ready to encounter the risen Christ in the breaking of bread, and once they recognize him, he disappears from sight. Thereafter, the disciples, and those following them, always stand in the shadow of the Cross: we stand stretching ahead towards the coming Christ, looking back to the Cross as the last publicly visible image in this world (the tomb being empty, after all, only seen by a few and needing interpretation). The "Passion," understood "in accordance with the scriptures," is the catalyst for reading scripture, and the whole of human existence and history, in a new manner, making everything new.

The crucified and exalted Lord, known in this way, is thus the starting point for reading scripture, the *hypothesis* in St Irenaeus' terms: it is this one about whom the scriptures speak—Moses wrote of him and himself prefigured him, he is the one speaking in the Psalms, and it is his glory that the prophets saw. The scriptures (meaning the Old Testament) thus form a treasury or a thesaurus for understanding the revelation of God in the person and Passion of Christ, the gospel. They form, again in St Irenaeus' terms, a mosaic, which, when read according to the right canon, portrays the King. The canon of truth, or the later creeds, articulate this hypothesis in particular historical contexts, against perceived aberrations, while tradition is the continuity of the proclamation of the gospel, the continuous contemplation of Christ through the reading of scripture, and succession is the visible expression of this continuity in the line of presbyters or bishops insofar as they do indeed maintain the right faith.

Focused on the person of the crucified and exalted Christ, the image of the invisible God, and guided by the Spirit bestowed by the risen Christ in our interpretation of the scriptures, we are brought into the identity of Christ, becoming his body—incarnating the Word—so that we can also call upon the one God as Abba, Father.

Such an approach can, again given all the limitations of pictorial representation, be represented by the sketch in figure 2 on page 175.

This reflection upon Christ according to the scriptures continues throughout subsequent history and has a history, *beginning with the Cross.*

There are all sorts of monuments to this tradition—patristic texts, conciliar decrees, liturgical rites, and artistic products—each of which has a certain value, to the extent that it is faithful to Christ, manifesting his truth in various contexts and ages. Treated historically, the apostolic writings are the first in this long series of monuments. But as written by the apostles and evangelists themselves, those who delivered the proclamation of Christ, they are qualitatively different. They can be examined historically—to investigate, for instance, the problems that Paul encountered in Corinth—but this is not to treat them *as scripture*: when treated as scripture, they are "detached" from (*our* reconstructions of) their "original meaning," to be part of the thesaurus or treasury of images utilized in proclaiming Christ, as, indeed, they are employed in the Church, whether as a short passage from which to proclaim the gospel or as part of the treasury of images used in hymnography to praise God for Christ in the Spirit.

When read from Genesis onwards, the scriptures do indeed have a narrative. One can, as it were, uncurl the circle in figure 2, extending it backwards to the moment of creation. This is what is often done when speaking of "salvation history," a term that has been used, as far as I am aware, only since the nineteenth century.[4] But, it is important to note, this "salvation history" is not "history" as that term is used in modern times, as a neutral, objective account of things "as they really were." Rather, it is a way of seeing the scriptures and their description of the world and its history in the light of Christ—it is a *confession*. The world did not come into being 4,004 years before Christ (as the calculations of James Ussher would have it based on the Old Testament genealogies), and "the Fall" is not a later event that can be correlated temporally, say, to the Battle of Troy. Rather, a properly theological cosmology and "history" of salvation—the economy or the plan of salvation—begins with the Passion of Christ, and from this vantage point looks backwards and forwards to see everything in this light. As it is from this perspective that we interpret creation and its history, we can even say that creation together with salvation was effected when Christ offered himself for the life of the world, on 25 March AD 33.

This "salvation history" is not co-extensive with our modern reconstructions of history: it was not the way that the disciples and apostles were reading scripture prior to the moment that the risen Christ opened the scriptures. The most that they hoped for was that the kingdom would be restored to Israel; what they were shown by Christ was that the whole of the human race lay in sin and death waiting to be restored, through death, to life. From their time with Jesus prior to the Passion, they did not understand him to be the Lord and could not answer those who said. "Is this not Joseph's son?" But in the light of the Passion, they could now proclaim that, in accordance with the scriptures, he is indeed the Son of God born of the Virgin, a nativity which, as we have seen, is described in terms of the Passion. Going back to the very beginning, we can now see that the instrument by which Christ brought order to the universe, creating the ordered and harmonious cosmos, is the Cross: it stands eternally still as the axis of the world, around which the cosmos rotates. Creation itself is indeed brought into being from nothing, *ex nihilo*, for nothing stands alongside the eternal God, independent of him; but the creation *ex nihilo* that Sts Irenaeus and Athanasius and others spoke of is precisely that created by our Lord and Savior, the crucified and risen Jesus Christ, the Coming One.

This "salvation history" also continues beyond the narrative described in scripture, in the depiction of the world and human beings in iconography and hagiography. Mary is now no longer merely a human mother, not understanding her son and trying to make human claims on him, but, already within the New Testament, she is the pure virgin who is obedient to God and conceives the Word. Subsequently, as the theological vision becomes ever broader, she is seen as the one miraculously conceived of barren parents, like the miraculous births in the Old Testament, and enters the temple, becoming identified with the temple as the one who contains God, and her death is seen as conforming to Christ's own exodus (with Thomas again appearing late on the scene). St Antony the Great, likewise, is no longer simply an ascetic teacher of (?Origenist) wisdom, as it might seem from historical study, but, in St Athanasius' theological vision, he is seen iconically, as the continuing presence of Christ on earth. Moreover, we are also invited to see ourselves in this light, to understand our own past as "salvation history," and so to continue the Incarnation of Christ by being reborn in the Virgin Mother, the Church, and ourselves becoming virgin mothers.

Such theology is not simply a matter of history, reconstructing things as we think they "really were," according to our canons and criteria of historical plausibility, but a witness to the transforming power of God manifest in Passion of Christ and extending to all of human existence, seen in the Word of God. To enter into this "premodern" way of doing theology requires us to abandon our "modern" pretensions. This is not to "demythologize" the Christian faith, for this faith was not mythological to begin with! It only appears to be so, when we forget how theology learned to speak, and we put its words in a modern framework. Nor can it be said that such an approach does not take "history" seriously. In fact, one might even say that it takes history more seriously than any modern historiography which attempts to describe "what really happened" while ignoring what happened later—believing that we can describe "what really happened" at the birth of Jesus from Mary, the history of Israel, or creation itself, as if the Passion had never occurred. The past no longer exists in itself, and any history is written from the perspective(s) of the present. Christian theology, on the other hand, is specifically a witness to the transforming power of God revealed in the Passion of Christ, the one who is still the Coming One, and invites all to see reality in him. One might describe the approach explored in this book as "a postmodern reappropriation of a premodern perspective," where "postmodern" does not mean the rejection of any claim to absolute truth, but only the rejection of (or liberation from) the "modern" claim to (its) "truth," recognizing instead that theology is the confession of the truth, Christ himself, who does not stand subject to any criterion other than himself, the Lord of all creation and its history.

NOTES

[1]Cf. St Augustine *On the Trinity* 3.1. Trans. E. Hill (Brooklyn, NY: New City Press, 1991).

[2]Cf. Peter Lombard, *Libri IV Sententiarum* 3.1.2; K. Rahner, "The Theology of the Incarnation," in *More Recent Writings*, Theological Investigations vol. 4 (Baltimore, MD: Helicon Press, 1966), 105–20, a profound reflection worthy of serious study.

[3]For a full examination see J. Behr, *The Nicene Faith* (Crestwood, NY: St Vladimir's Seminary, 2004).

[4]The language of "salvation history" (*Heilsgeschichte*) seems to have originated with the nineteenth-century Erlangen School, and especially J. C. K. von Hofmann, see for instance, his *Weissagung und Erfüllung im Alten und Neuen Testament* (2 parts; Nördlingen: C. H. Beck, 1841–44).

Index